Pieroni's Fountain

PIERONI'S FOUNTAIN

An Italian Immigrant's Search for Respectability in Victorian Bath

Colin Fisher

AKEMAN
PRESS

Published by AKEMAN PRESS
www.akemanpress.com

ISBN 978-0-9560989-6-2

Printed by Berforts Information Press, Stevenage

CONTENTS

1

SIGNOR STEFANO VALLERIO PIERONI
A Forgotten Bath character

Bath has witnessed many people who became known as characters. They ranged from Beau Nash, Georgian Bath's rakish master of ceremonies, to Guinea Pig Jack, an Italian newspaper seller and street entertainer, who died in 1907, and whose trick was exhibiting performing Guinea Pigs.[1] There is one character however, a contemporary of Guinea Pig Jack and also an Italian, who has been largely forgotten. His name was Stefano Vallerio Pieroni and he lived and worked in Bath as a plaster-figure maker and modeller from 1848 till his death in 1900.

There are a few reminders of Pieroni still to be found in Bath. The most imposing is the fountain on what is popularly known as Bog Island. It was not originally located there, but in the semi-circle at the end of Bath Street facing the Roman Baths. It carries the grand inscription, Stefano Vallerio Pieroni fecit 1859. It is now topped by an urn but originally it was crowned by a statue of King Bladud, the legendary founder of Bath. The statue is now in Parade Gardens where it is accompanied by a stone carving of a pig. It was whilst looking after his pigs, before he became king, that Bladud, in the fable, discovered Bath's hot springs. There is also, just within the entrance to Royal Victoria Park, a large carved shallow stone bowl, known as a tazza, set on a plinth. This was donated by Pieroni, and in a slanting light the letters SSV, standing for Signor Stefano Vallerio, can just be seen carved on the pedestal.[2] Few probably note these palimpsests of Pieroni's presence in Bath.

Pieroni arrived in England as an itinerant seller of plaster figures, a figurinai in Italian. When he settled in Bath he gave much effort to becoming recognised and respected within the town. The building of the mineral water fountain was part of that effort. Pieroni's successes and failures in his search for social acceptance were paralleled by the praise and contempt that the town alternately expressed for the fountain. Both Pieroni and the fountain were part of a continuous debate in nineteenth-century Bath about the city's role as a spa. Some argued that, as a spa city, Bath should have many grand fountains, but others were unwilling to pay

Opposite: The tazza in Royal Victoria Park, with Pieroni's name now barely legible for such extravagances through the rates. When fountains were built they caused arguments about whether they were beautiful or ugly and about the nuisance of maintaining them. The stories of Pieroni and his fountain also involve many other aspects of the social, commercial and political life of Victorian Bath.

When Stefano Pieroni died the *Bath Journal* wrote:

> By the death of Mr Pieroni a well-known figure disappears from our midst. He possessed a striking individuality and his striking appearance immediately portrayed that he was the possessor of an artistic temperament.[3]

His artistic bent was expressed in his 'rare ability' as a plaster-figure maker and a sculptor, and, according to the *Bath Chronicle*, 'in his prime Mr Pieroni was a man who enjoyed considerable popularity in the city'.[4] He had been for a long period a familiar presence and was 'remarkably clever as a sculptor'. Another writer, in a later remembrance, recalled that Pieroni was 'a very fine specimen of his countrymen'[5]. It was also said that he had made a fortune during his time in Bath but had died in obscurity and poverty.[6]

His appearance alone, it seems, was enough to make Signor Pieroni (he always used the Italian honorific) a noticeable presence in the city. He had a flowing white beard and wore a broad brimmed, 'wide-awake' hat and frock coat.[7] One newspaper reported that 'he was possessed of a fine figure and striking face and he was a distinct personality.'[8] Several portraits were painted of him. John Egerton of Milsom Street exhibited a portrait of Pieroni, 'whose figure is well known to Bathonians' at the Royal Academy Summer Exhibition in 1899. He donated it to the newly-opened Victoria Art Gallery in 1900, where it was acquisition no. 17 and was described as 'a very fine portrait'.[9] Sibyl Hippesley, who lived in Great Pulteney Street, and belonged to the family that owned the Ston Easton estate, also painted a picture of Pieroni which was exhibited at the Victoria Art Gallery. Both of these paintings disappeared from the gallery's collection sometime before 1974.[10] There was another portrait painted by Mrs Preston King and exhibited in 1899 at the Bath Sketch Club and at the Bath and West County Show held at Lyncombe Vale.[11] Whether this painting is still in existence is not known. In 1866 Pieroni agreed a deal with a painter called Vichery, whereby, in return for making a bust of Vichery, he would receive a portrait of himself. The two friends fell out, as we shall see later, and the portrait was never painted.[12] There must have been photographs of Pieroni, but so far I have found none. There is, however, a photograph of Ferdinando Mazzei, who sported the look favoured by figurinai, with beard and broad-brimmed hat, which gives an idea how Pieroni may have looked. Mazzei was an Italian figure

A photograph of Ferdinando Mazzei with some of his plaster casts

maker, born in Tuscany around 1821, who emigrated to Britain, living first in London and later in Cardiff. He had two brothers, Giovanni and Pellegrino, who were also figure makers. Giovanni lived and worked in Bath for a few years, at 4 Bridewell Lane and later at Avon Street, until his death in 1872.[13] He must have known Pieroni.

The aim of this study is not only to revive the memory of a forgotten character but also to explore how an immigrant who began as a lowly street trader managed to gain a place in Bath society, although perhaps not as grand a position as he had hoped for. The ambition to improve their lot is a common one amongst immigrants, and there were many other Italian plaster-figure makers who travelled to Britain with the same hope. Several of them were also called Pieroni. Pietro Pieroni settled in London, Nicholas Pieroni settled in Liverpool, while Adolfo and Rafaelle Pieroni established themselves in Bristol. Rafaelle is a typical example of a figure maker who made good. He was born in Tuscany about 1854, but by 1881 was working in Bristol as one of eight Italian plaster-figure makers under a foreman called Lorenzo D'Prato. These figure makers not only worked for D'Prato but were also boarders in his house. Rafaelle managed to start working for himself, however, and by 1889 had established a plaster-figure making business called R Pieroni & Co at Perry Road in Bristol. By that time, however, the market for plaster busts and statuettes was declining and, like many of his fellow figurinai, he turned to selling ice cream and confectionary in his sweet shop in the Hotwells Road. Three years later he seems to have given up modelling altogether to concentrate on his confectionery business.[14] Stefano Pieroni, however, set his social ambitions rather higher than Rafaelle. He wanted to be a recognised figure in Bath.

2

FROM TUSCANY TO BATH

Stefano Vallerio Pieroni was born in 1819 in Gragnano, a small hamlet near the city of Lucca in Tuscany. At that time his birthplace was within the Duchy of Lucca, which had only been formed four years earlier at the Congress of Vienna, after the dispossession of Napoleon's younger sister Elisa Bonaparte whom he had made Duchess of Lucca. Stefano's father, Vallerio, was sometimes described by his sons as a merchant and sometime as a farmer.[15] It is unlikely that he was well off or his sons would not have needed to emigrate.

Italian Immigrants – Figure Makers & Organ Grinders

Gragnano is only a few miles north east of Lucca in the foothills of the Apennines. In these mountains the conditions for agriculture were poor and there was a long tradition of people emigrating to find work to supplement their families' incomes. In some districts, such as the area around Gragnano and further north in Borgo Val di Toro, Barga and Compiano, the agricultural situation was better but still not productive enough to support families alone. From these districts, in the early nineteenth century, had travelled across the Alps the groups of

> poor Italian boys that frequent our [English] streets selling images, playing organs or exhibiting monkeys, land tortoises and white mice.[16]

The last occupation prefigures Guinea Pig Jack exhibiting his guinea pigs in Bath later in the nineteenth century.

It was, as the *Penny Magazine* of 1833 put it,

> a curious fact that each district has, and has had for many generations, its peculiar profession and line of emigration, never interfering with those of another district.[17]

The district which Stefano Pieroni and his brother Pietro – who was born about 1817 – came from must have specialised in the making

An Italian hawker of plaster figures from John Thomas Smith's *Etchings of Remarkable Beggars, Itinerant Traders and Other Persons*, 1815

THE ITALIAN ORGAN GRINDERS AS A NUISANCE

The organ grinders, or hurdy-gurdy men, were the least respectable of the Italian immigrants. The urban middle classes of the 1850s and 1860s found their music unpalatable, and a nuisance when it was played in the streets outside their homes. Their dislike was heightened by the fact that the Italians' music was appreciated by the working classes and the poor. Charles Babbage, the mathematician and designer of a proto-computer, was one of those who led a campaign for legislation against the organ grinders' noise. Babbage claimed that his work was disturbed by the organ grinders' disturbances and that a quarter of his time was 'consumed by the hindrances occasioned by street bands'. In 1864 he wrote in a pamphlet:

> *The great encouragers of street music belong chiefly to the lower classes of society. Of these, the frequenters of public houses and beer shops patronise the worst and most noisy kinds of music ... It not infrequently gives rise to a dance by little ragged urchins and sometimes by half intoxicated men who occasionally accompany the noise with their own discordant voices ... Another class, who are great supporters of street music, consists of ladies of elastic virtues and cosmopolitan tendencies to whom it affords a decent excuse for displaying their fascinations at their own open windows.*

There was no legislation forthcoming and the numbers of street musicians continued to grow, from 872 in 1871 to 1,441 in 1891. Street musicians seemed not to be a big problem in Bath. There are only a few incidents recorded in the *Bath Chronicle*. In 1845 Joseph Manuel, an itinerant organ grinder, was accused of assaulting a boy called Vaughan. In 1854 an Italian organ grinder 'with an un-spellable name' was found guilty of obstruction by exhibiting a monkey in Rivers Street and causing a crowd to appear. Some were charmed by the Italian manners of the organ grinders. One correspondent to the *Bath Chronicle*

> *heard a well-dressed lady exclaim as she reluctantly turned away from the spot where [an Italian organ grinder] was breaking Donizetti upon the wheel, 'he must be a gentleman – his manners are so very superior!' She had just presented him with five shillings, which he had accepted with a languid condescension very touching to behold.*

This gentleman argued that the German brass street bands were causing more musical distress, to those of discerning musical tastes, than the organ grinders. These German bands took up their places in the best streets of the upper town. They were 'nomadic nerve crushers [who] inflicted their torture on us with impunity' by disturbing the inhabitants of the houses who might be ill, trying to do work, read their novels or practise their own music-making that required mental effort.'

and selling of plaster figures because they both became figurinai. The area around Lucca had long been famous for plaster statues, mostly religious ones for devotional use. By the nineteenth century, however, the repertoire had expanded. In 1817 one figurinai called Tomei sold his stock in trade of 300 moulds used for making medals, candelabra and statuettes of, among others, Apollo, Bacchus, Socrates, Generals Wellington and Blucher and Pope Leo. Perhaps the most famous model sold by the figurinai however was the gatti lucchessi, the cat of Lucca that, because of its simple shape, was easy to model.[18]

There was a well-established routine for travelling plaster-figure makers. Groups of eight or twelve were formed of a bunch of young boys overseen by an older capo. The capo was the person who made the plaster casts, and possibly some of the moulds, and the boys would go out into the towns and villages through which they passed carrying a board with pegs on their heads onto which the plaster models were fixed. Their job was to sell as many as possible. As the group headed north from Lucca they would send their moulds and working tools on ahead by wagon to the next city and follow on by foot. When they arrived, they would source the materials they needed, make more casts and remain until they had sold their stock or saturated the market. They would then move on to the next town. Many, such as Stefano and Pietro Pieroni, got as far as

Boys at a roadside alehouse by James Collinson, 1849

England; others went to France, Germany or the Low Countries. They might travel for a number of years but most intended to return to Lucca with the money they had saved. Many of the boys were on three-year contracts with the capos and at the end of that time they would start up in business on their own.

Many people considered the figure sellers to be vagrants. At least one English writer, however, thought well of them:

> Those among them who are vendors of images by selling for a few pence the plaster casts of the great and the good and casts from ancient works of art, may pretend to the dignity of trading, and may even have the merit of improving and propagating a taste for the fine arts ... As a body if they are to be held as vagrants they must be considered as the most inoffensive and amusing of vagrants.[19]

The figure makers had a little more status than the organ grinders who were largely seen as a nuisance.

The plaster-figure sellers, in contrast, were often viewed in an affectionate and even romantic light as seen in James Collinson's painting of Italian 'image boys' selling their wares in a country pub.

Stefano Pieroni Arrives in England

Stefano Pieroni arrived in Dover in on 13 November 1837 in company with Nicholas Pellostrini. They had travelled from Ostend on the packet ship 'Widgeon' and were both described as image makers.[20] His brother Pietro Pieroni arrived in England nearly nine years later in September 1846.

It is perhaps significant that Stefano was 18 years old when he arrived in Dover and was travelling with a single companion. He was probably too old to be one of the boys employed to sell plaster models, and they in any case tended to travel in larger groups. For example, an Antonio Pieroni arrived in England in 1839 and again in 1852 and on both occasions he was in a group of around ten figure makers.[21] Perhaps, on his arrival in England, Stefano Pieroni had already served an apprenticeship with a group of figurinai when he was younger, or maybe he came from a family of established moulders and modellers and had learned his trade from them. There were a number of Pieronis well known in the trade in Tuscany. Adolfo Pieroni, who was born in Lucca in 1832 and lived until 1890, was an established sculptor and medallist working in Florence and specialising in portrait medals.[22] In 1855 a model of the Coliseum by Dr Emil Braun and a Roman architect called Francesco Pieroni was on display in the Crystal Palace in London.[23] It seems probable that Stefano was a trained modeller, and not a street hawker, when he arrived in England, and was ready to start to build a name and a career for himself.

At first Stefano went to London, as did many Italian immigrants. Most settled in the 'Little Italy' area of Hatton Garden and Saffron Hill in Holborn. In 1851 in Holborn there were 92 figure makers, 79 picture frame makers and 178 street musicians and organ grinders, all of Italian origin.[24] The Italian immigrants were mostly poor and lived in overcrowded lodging houses run by other Italians. The figure makers however, more so than the organ grinders, tended to work in family groups with the women of the family working in crafts such as paper-flower making. There was, for example, Nicoli Pieroni recorded living at 2 Leather Lane in Hatton Garden in 1841. He was a figure maker living in a household of ten others, one of whom was also a figure maker, while the others were flower makers.[25] It is quite possible that Stefano Pieroni settled into one of these households and learned to speak English. We cannot be certain though because he cannot be traced in the 1841 census.

Life could be difficult for the figure sellers. In 1843 Antonio Caponi of Grays Inn Road in London was taken to court and accused of selling a plaster cast of a naked female figure in the street, seemingly a great offence against Victorian primness.[26] Other young image sellers could be lured into trouble. In Birmingham in 1859 a young Italian figure maker was 'inveigled into a den of iniquity' by a 17-year-old prostitute. Once inside, the young woman was joined by an older woman and together they beat him up and stole £3 14s from him.[27] In 1876 it was reported that a poor Italian figure maker in Belfast had been visiting the Belfast Skin hospital for treatment for a sore leg. He could not afford to pay for the treatment and so offered the doctor a plaster cast of Dickens which was 'all the poor fellow had to offer'.[28]

Despite the harsh conditions, many figure makers worked their way up from street-selling to owning shops. Giovanni Bianchi, for instance, arrived in London and then moved to Norwich where he married a local girl and set up shop as a figure maker, sculptor and artist until his death in 1872.[29] Some, like Antonio Caponi remained in London but developed their business from street trading to something more respectable. In 1851 Antonio was a member of company of twelve Italian figure makers living in a crowded tenement under a master called Domenico Caponi. Later, Antonio was joined by his older brother Luigi and together they managed their own team of figure makers and sellers. They had improved the quality of their products and decreased their reliance on street hawking to the extent that they were listed in the London trade directories.[30]

Stefano Pieroni made a similar transition. In 1843 he was no longer in the Holborn area but was living on the Kingsland Road in the East End of London. On Christmas day that year he married Rebekah Moore at the church of St John the Baptist, Shoreditch. Rebekah had been born in Norwich and was the daughter of a carpenter.[31] Pieroni described himself on the marriage certificate as an artist and so clearly saw himself as having risen above the ranks of both image moulder and image hawker. Around 1849 he moved to Bath. He presumably thought that a genteel and relatively prosperous city such as Bath would provide a good market for his figurative products. It is possible that when he first arrived in Bath he worked as a dyer rather than a figure maker. The Bath Directory for 1850 lists a Pieroni and Elliott, dyers, at 26 Broad Street. There was no such entry in the 1849 Directory nor in the next one, published in 1852, which lists Pieroni as a figure maker at 4 Bath Street.[32]

There had already been at least one other Italian figure maker and plaster manufacturer in Bath by this time. John Anthony Tognieri, who came from Tuscany, was living on Terrace Walk in 1833 and was described as an 'Italian artist in models', available to make plaster masks from 'living or deceased busts' or busts and figures for holding gas lights. These were all services later provided by Pieroni. Peter Malone has suggested that Pieroni acquired Tognieri's stock-in-trade and moulds when Tognieri experienced financial problems after 1845.[33] By 1851 Tognieri had left Bath and was living in Holborn, although his wife was still in the city. If he had been in London a few years earlier, he may well have met Stefano Pieroni and encouraged him to move to Bath. By 1861 Tognieri had retired to Bath where he died in 1870.[34]

Stefano and Rebekah Pieroni settled in Bath and in 1858 Stefano became a naturalised British citizen after four referees declared him to be 'a person of respectability and good character and well affected towards Her Majesty'.[35] Stefano retained his links with London, however, through his brother Pietro who continued to work as a figure maker in the Holborn area. Pietro married Patty Frost at St Pauls, Bunhill in London and they had four children, all born in Holborn. Stefano and Rebekah, however, never had any children.

With his arrival in Bath, and his naturalisation as a British subject in 1858, Stefano Pieroni had begun his search for respectability in his adopted city.

3

SIGNOR PIERONI, MODELLER AND MOULDER

In the 1851 census Pieroni was living at 4 Bath Street. The premises were occupied by four households and Pieroni's consisted of himself, his wife, his servant Dominic Maconi, who was also a figure maker from Tuscany, and a lodger called John Mills, a sculptor from Edgbaston.[36] Bath Street was a good address as the street linked the Pump Room and Abbey Church Yard with the Hot and Cross Baths, although the yards and stables of the White Hart Inn, just to the north, may have lowered the tone somewhat, as they were notorious as a hang-out of prostitutes and ne'er-do-wells.[37]

It is likely that Maconi and Mills worked with Pieroni in his figure-making business. By 1854 Pieroni's workshop and studio were in Parsonage Lane, where he continued to be based as long as he was in business. In 1854 Pieroni advertised himself as a moulder and modeller in plaster and French composition.[38] He had the busts of nearly 100 famous men in stock, including lawyers such as Coke and Hale. He also made busts and death masks to order, and sold garden vases and statuary made of artificial stone and figures used as stands for gas lights.

SIGNOR PIERONI,

FIGURE MANUFACTURER,

MODELLER and MOULDER

IN PLASTER AND FRENCH COMPOSITION.

Figures and Alabaster cleaned and repaired. Vases and Statues, in Artificial Stone, for Gardens. Figures for Gas, from 1 to 7 feet high. A fine Collection of upwards of 100 Busts of the most celebrated Men. Masks taken from Life or Death. Busts executed.

Studio—PARSONAGE LANE,

Residence—4, BATH STREET, BATH.

Pieroni's advertisement in the *Bath Post Office Directory* for 1854

Parsonage Lane

Pieroni's first studio in Parsonage Lane was at the north-west end, on land owned by, and adjacent to, a set of Commercial Rooms that provided a meeting place for local tradesmen and businessmen.[39] Pieroni would have used the Commercial Rooms to meet friends and talk with clients. In 1859, when the Commercial Rooms were demolished and replaced by an extension to the General Hospital, Pieroni moved his studio to the southern end of Parsonage Lane.[40]

Before 1889 Pieroni's workshop was at 11 Parsonage Lane, which he shared with a chimney sweep, an upholsterer, a banjo maker, a French polisher, a wood turner and a printer.[41]

He also had a studio at 13 Parsonage Lane, which he moved into sometime after 1889. This may explain one of Bath's architectural curiosities. At the

The Commercial Rooms, on the corner of Parsonage Lane and Upper Borough Walls, was demolished in 1859 to make way for an extension to the Mineral Water Hospital. It was built as the rectory for Bath Abbey between 1786 and 1793, on the site of an earlier rectory, which itself stood on the site of the parsonage of St Mary de Stalls. It became the Commercial Rooms around 1836, when the rector moved to Rock House on Lansdown. Although the building's architect is not known, its style suggests that it was almost certainly Thomas Baldwin, who, as city architect, undertook a major programme of city improvements between 1775 and 1792. This engraving, by Henry Sargant Storer, appeared in Pierce Egan's *Walks Through Bath*, published in 1819, and shows the building when it was still a rectory.

Architectural curiosties in Parsonage Lane, which may have adorned the entrance to Pieroni's studio

southern end of the lane, on the west side, are three odd features: a door frame surrounded by egg-and-dart moulding, a large round arched window (now blocked up), also with egg-and-dart moulding, and a blank, Palladian-style double window frame surmounted by two putti supporting a wreath and an armorial shell, again surrounded by egg-and-dart mouldings. The window with the putti is on the side wall of 33 Westgate Street but the door and the large window are part of the first house on the lane. This was probably Pieroni's workshop and shop at no. 13, with architectural embellishments designed by Pieroni himself. Egg-and-dart moulding is normally used for cornices rather than doors and cartouches, and the solecism of these designs reflects the naivety of someone such as Pieroni with no formal architectural training. The similarity between the putti on the window frame and the figures of the four seasons on Pieroni's fountain of 1859 (illustrated on page 34) is another reason for attributing them to Pieroni. The door would have been the entrance to the workshop, the round headed window the shop window, and the rectangular window a showcase for advertising posters. Although the building with the door and large window is now 1 Parsonage Lane there is reason

HARRINGTON PLACE
QUEEN STREET
OLD BOND STREET
NEW BOND STREET PLACE
BURTON
TRIM
STREET
BOROUGH
GASCOYNE PLACE
Blue Coat School
Commercial Rooms
NORTHUM
SAWCLOSE
LANE
STREET
Chapel
BRIDEWELL
PARSONAGE
UNION
UNION PASSAGE
CHEAP
WESTGATE
STREET
CROSS BATH LANE
ABBEY C
Pump Room
Royal Baths
CHANDOS BUILDINGS
BATH
STREET
STALL
STREET
Cross Bath
St Johns Hospital
CHAPEL COURT
Chapel
Tepid Baths
St Catharines Hospital
HETLING COURT

to believe that before renumbering this was the last building in Parsonage Lane – no. 13.[42]

Parsonage Lane was one of Bath's original thoroughfares, laid out when King Alfred re-established the city in the ninth century. It was named after a vicarage, provided for the incumbent of the long-vanished church of St Mary de Stalls, that once stood at the top of the lane.[43] By the nineteenth century, Parsonage Lane was a rather disreputable back alley, but it was where Isaac Pitman, the inventor of Pitman Shorthand, had his Phonetic Institute for 20 years between 1855 and 1875. These were the years when Pieroni was most active in the lane. Pitman gave the following description of the place:

> It is the only filthy lane I have seen in this clean and beautiful city of crescents and squares, and the pollution is not physical alone, but moral also, for on the other side of the narrow lane two or three steps from my office door the 'social evil' festers.[44]

The physical pollution Pitman referred to came largely from several slaughterhouses in the lane:

> Close to the street entrance [of the institute] is a slaughter house and underneath and around and about it are the necessary appliances for keeping, killing and cutting up sheep and cows for a large butcher's business. A more unsavoury entrance to a business premises, I think, does not exist in the city. Although the refuse from the slaughtered animals is generally removed every 3 or 4 days, it is sometimes allowed to accumulate for a longer period and the smell thence arising is extremely offensive.[45]

There was also a brewery in the lane which would have added variety to the stinks of the slaughterhouse. Such a noisome and dark alley was also a likely site for crime. The butcher's shop at the bottom of the lane fronted onto Westgate Street but the work rooms at the back connected to an iron trapdoor in the lane that was simply held down by its own weight. In February 1862 William Wyatt, one of the butcher's employees, used this means to enter the building and steal some money. The butcher heard a disturbance and went downstairs but could not see anyone. A passing police constable, however, saw Wyatt emerging from the trapdoor and arrested him. He was given three year's penal servitude.[46]

The Figure-making Business

Although Pieroni had become a naturalised British citizen, he continued to refer to himself as Signor Pieroni in his advertisements, presumably because the exoticism of an Italian honorific was a good marketing ploy

Opposite: A detail from Cotterell's 1852-53 map of Bath showing the area around Parsonage Lane and Bath Street

Left: Casts from the sculptures on the west front of Bath Abbey, possibly by Pieroni, now stored in the chapel of the Abbey burial ground. The figure in the central photograph is one of the angels climbing Jacob's Ladder

for his business of selling figures in plaster, marble and alabaster. His moulding and casting work extended to architectural commissions. In 1859 he restored the Coat of Arms over the front door of Bellott's Hospital when it was rebuilt.[47] In 1865 he made moulds and castings for building and decorative work in the new Bridgwater town hall.[48] It was said that he 'enjoyed considerable reputation for the skill he possessed in preparing moulds for building and decorative purposes and for statues'. The suggestion has been made by Peter Malone that Pieroni may have been involved in taking casts of the surviving sculptures on the west front of Bath Abbey as part of the restoration undertaken by Gilbert Scott between 1864 and 1867.[49] These casts are currently stored in the chapel of the old Abbey burial ground. It cannot be proved that Pieroni did this work but it is clear that he had the capability of doing it.

Pieroni often had partners and employees. For some time he worked with William Hy Vivian and his son, who later set up on their own account as plaster moulders in Corn Street.[50] Pieroni also worked with amateur modellers such as Mr Broadhurst, a Bath dentist.

Working as a modeller and moulder had its dangers. In 1858 a man was cleaning the inside of the windows in Pieroni's studio in Parsonage Lane when his ladder gave way 'and precipitated him amongst a quantity of statuary. He was picked out from amongst the arms, legs and trunks of the goods he had demolished – uninjured'.[51] There were also greater dangers. In 1854 a building in Parsonage Lane caught fire. Flames were seen at three o'clock in the morning and the police, the watermen and the City Engineer were soon on the scene tackling the blaze, which they succeeded in preventing from spreading to nearby buildings. The fire had started in the premises of Mr Offer, a cabinet maker, but the building was also occupied by Mr Davis, another cabinet maker, Mr Banks, a carver and gilder, and Pieroni. They lost all their stock and their tools, but whereas Mr Offer had some insurance none of the others did.[52] This was the first of several financial crises that marked Pieroni's career. However, on this occasion he seems to have recovered quickly because in a few years he was beginning his expensive fountain project.

Fire was a persistent risk in figure-maker's workshops. In 1888, at Raffaelle Pieroni's figure-making workshop in Perry Road, Bristol, one of the workmen, Pietro Regani ,was mixing paint on a stove. Adolpho Pieroni, who was in a different room, heard Pietro scream and, when he ran in, he found Pietro in flames and was himself severely burned trying to douse them. Pietro later died and this was recorded as an accidental death caused by the paint mixture boiling over and catching alight.[53] It is

An advertisment from the 1861 Bath Post Office Directory

highly probable that both Rafaelle and Adolpho were related to Stefano Pieroni, though not as brothers because they were much younger than Stefano.

Captain Speke's Bust

Taking death masks was an important part of Pieroni's business and in 1864 he had the opportunity to make the death mask of a famous figure, Captain John Hanning Speke. Speke had accompanied Sir Richard Burton on an expedition to Somalia between 1854 and 1855 and again on an expedition to find the source of the Nile between 1857 and 1859. Speke and Burton jointly discovered Lake Tanganyika, while Speke, who made a separate foray, also discovered Lake Victoria, which he claimed to be the source of the Nile. Between 1860 and 1863, this time in the company of Captain Grant, Speke made a return journey to Lake Victoria and became further convinced that it was the Nile's source. Burton, however, disagreed, and the two men entered into an antagonistic debate. The British Association for the Advancement of Science was due to hold its annual meeting at Bath in September 1864 and the geographical section organised a debate between Burton and Speke on the source of the Nile. The debate, scheduled for Thursday 16 September, attracted much attention. Speke came down to Bath and stayed at his uncle's estate at Neston Park, about seven miles from the city. On the afternoon before the debate, Speke went out on the estate with his nephew to shoot partridge. At about 4pm, as he was climbing over a low wall, his shotgun went off. He was severely wounded and died within fifteen minutes. At the inquest the following Friday, a verdict of accidental death was returned.[54] Since then there has been speculation about whether Speke's death was suicide motivated by anxiety over the coming debate with Burton. The most recent work on the exploration of the Nile argues that the death was clearly accidental. The rumour that it was a suicide to prevent his views being trounced in debate by Burton was probably untrue, although Burton himself thought it might be, and blamed himself for Speke's death.[55]

It was reported on 22 September that Mr Hill of Wood Street, a carver, gilder and picture-frame maker, had been commissioned by Speke's family to prepare a bust of the deceased explorer. He was assisted by Signor Pieroni who had taken Speke's death mask, and it was reported that the cast had 'been carefully and skilfully executed'. Hill paid Pieroni £4 19s for the work.[56] Hill then commissioned Louis Gardie, a French sculptor, to make the bust.[57] Gardie, who was 67 years old, had exhibited at the Royal Academy and at the Great Exhibition of 1851, before moving from London to Bath with his wife, and in 1861 he was living in a tenement in Westgate Buildings.[58] In October and November 1864 he advertised that

SEARCHING FOR PIERONI'S BUST OF SPEKE

There are several surviving busts of Captain Speke but identifying one of them as by Pieroni is not easy. The difficulty of locating any of Pieroni's busts of Speke shows how far into obscurity Pieroni's reputation has fallen. The plaster bust in the National Portrait Gallery collection is by Louis Gardie, who made two busts of Speke. One of Gardie's busts shows Speke wearing a bush shirt under a tartan plaid draped over his left shoulder; the other shows him bare chested except for the tartan.[63] It was this later version, completed in 1865, that was cast in bronze. The entry on Speke in the *Oxford Dictionary of National Biography* records the existence of a plaster bust of Speke by RG Pieroni in the Royal Albert Memorial Museum in Exeter.[64] Unfortunately the museum reports that they have no record of such a bust.[65] The Royal Geographical Society also had a plaster bust of Speke by Pieroni at one time, but, although they have a bronze cast of the Gardie bust made by the Coalbrookdale Company, which they acquired in 1931, the Pieroni bust has disappeared, possibly being disposed of because it compared unfavourably with the bronze bust.[66] Another bust of Speke forms part of his memorial in his family's ancestral church of St Andrew in the village of Dowlish Wake, where he was buried. This bust is different to Gardie's, but is made from marble and so cannot be by Pieroni.[67] Pieroni's bust is still a mystery and no copies are known to have survived. The story of Speke's death mask, and the various busts made subsequently, is further complicated by a claim by Edgar Papworth who sculpted a marble bust of Speke in the Shire Hall in Taunton. Isabel Burton reported that Papworth had told her and Richard Burton that he 'only took the cast' {of Speke] after his death and asked whether he had managed a good likeness.[68]

One of Louis Gardie's busts of Speke

Although it has not been possible to identify any surviving examples of Pieroni's bust of Speke, at least in public collections, it seems certain that they did once exist.

his bust of Speke would soon be completed and could be seen at Mr Hill's shop in Wood Street. It was finished by the middle of November and was a very good likeness according to those who knew Captain Speke.[59] On 6 and 13 October, however, Pieroni placed a notice in the *Bath Chronicle* declaring that he had received several applications for busts of the late Captain Speke and 'will have ready in a few days a life-sized bust modelled from the original mask' taken by himself. Each bust would be priced at one guinea. Gardie retaliated with an advertisement of his own:

> Louis Gardie begs to caution the public against imitation busts [obviously those sold by Pieroni] which have been advertised for sale, as being made from the original mask, such being incorrect, the original being in the possession of Mr Hill and being the property of the family.[60]

It seems that Pieroni was using his access to the death mask to produce an unauthorised bust. But Gardie's bust was not a total success. In November he advertised that the Speke family had approved the bust, although one family member rejected it – this subject will be returned to later. Gardie started on a second bust, to meet the family's revised requirements, which was completed, and cast in bronze at Coalbrookdale, in early summer 1865.[61]

In December 1864, Pieroni exhibited his bust of Speke – complete with pedestal – at an 'Industrial Exhibition' organised by Working Men's Hospital Fund Committee. So, despite Gardie's protestations, Pieroni was still producing his version of Speke's bust. The *Bath Chronicle* thought that the exhibition had been poorly organised and that most of the exhibits were 'the trifling results of leisure hours'. These included a model of a cemetery, several models of Clifton suspension bridge and a portable picnic seat. There were also curiosities such as Chinese spectacles and the skull of a dodo on display.

Pieroni also exhibited a bust of Mr Venables, one of the exhibition's adjudicators, which may have influenced the decision to award him a medal for the bust of Speke. When the mayor presented the medal, however, a heckler shouted that Pieroni should not receive it and should be asked whether he had modelled the figure or whether it had been done 'by a poor man who might now be living in a garret'. The heckler was hissed, the mayor said that they were all proud to have amongst them an Italian with so much talent and Pieroni was warmly applauded.[62] This is the first hint that Pieroni was not unwilling to claim credit for work that, at the least, involved the labours of others. In 1868, the Taunton Courier and Western Advertiser reported that Pieroni's bust of Speke was on display in the British Museum, but perhaps this was just advertising hype promoting the facsimiles of the bust which could be had from Mr Jeboult's shop in the High Street.

Making and selling plaster figures was a financially precarious business. Most practitioners went bankrupt at some stage in their careers and by 1863 Pieroni was in serious difficulties. He owed money to Obadiah Jones, a baker, John Line, a carpenter, Nathaniel Wilcocks, a brass founder, Henry Eve, an auctioneer, and others. They pressed him for payment, but agreed to accept payment of five shillings in the pound (25%) in settlement. Pieroni signed a deed of composition which meant that he avoided being declared a bankrupt.[69] Whether the creditors agreed to the settlement because they had some sympathy with a fellow small businessman or because they thought little would be gained by forcing him into bankruptcy is not known. Pieroni's financial problems reflected the decline in demand for plaster casts in the second half of the nineteenth century. Indeed, by the end of the century plaster figures were out of fashion and the market was largely confined to souvenirs sold at seaside resorts.[70] Consequently, like many other figure makers, Pieroni tried his hand at other businesses. In the deed of composition, Pieroni was described not only as a modeller but also as a wine merchant, but that story that will be told later.

4

THE MINERAL WATER FOUNTAIN
Politics and Hot Water

In 1859, Stefano Pieroni unveiled his reworking of the mineral water fountain that had stood at the junction of Bath Street and Stall Street since 1856. A general election had also been held in 1859, when Bath had to elect its two members of parliament, and during the campaign the old fountain became a target for satire and political rhetoric. The changes Pieroni made to the fountain, and his decision to top it with a statue of Bladud, had political and symbolic as well as architectural significance. Pieroni's involvement with the fountain, and its political significance, can only be understood by telling the story of how the fountain came to be built in the first place.

The 1856 Fountain

It begins in the early 1850s when Bath experienced a mild form of fountain mania. Many of the proposals were hopelessly over-ambitious. One plan was to have a series of fountains cascading down from Lansdown, with fountains in St James's Square, below the Royal Crescent and near the obelisk in Royal Victoria Park.[71] However problems with the water supply led to the plans being scaled down and eventually abandoned in 1851 when the public's attention turned to the forthcoming Great Exhibition.

In 1855, however the focus of fountain mania switched to the idea of having a fountain in the city centre that would dispense, and advertise, Bath's famous hot mineral water. This was possible because an engineer called James Williams had installed in York Street a steam engine for pumping water from the Queen's Bath. In September 1855 the residents of Abbey Church Yard asked the council for permission to build a hot water fountain in the Church Yard. This was approved in principle and a Hot Water Fountain Committee was formed with Williams as secretary.[72] A competition was set up to choose a design. Not everyone thought the idea a good one and Walter Savage Landor, who lived in Bath between 1838 and 1864, published a mock design for the fountain featuring a naked statue of King Bladud sheltering under an umbrella and surrounded by Bath chairs and pigs.
In the pamphlet accompanying the design he wrote:

> This design has been published at the request of a numerous and admiring circle of friends, who are of the opinion that an enlightened

public cannot fail to appreciate its beauty and fitness as an embellishment to the western front of our time honoured and venerable abbey.

What though the dream of Bishop King be lost in spray

Is it not right that the barbarous attempts of our ancestors should be swamped on the triumphant tide of modern improvement, even as the Roman temple gave way to Gothic pile.

As the public are so enlightened, it can hardly be necessary to explain our design.

Bladud prince of Chairmen is represented risen from his bath with health renewed. And tears of gratitude dripping from his patent German umbrella, while his happy aerated pigs frolic around him and participate in his joy.[73]

Walter Savage Landor's mock design for a hot water fountain

As we shall see, the fountain that was built by Pieroni in 1859 featured a statue of Bladud. Whether Landor's lampoon was triggered by a design submitted by Pieroni for the 1855 competition, or whether the cartoon inspired Pieroni to incorporate Bladud in his later design, we do not know.

Eventually two designs were shortlisted, both by James Palmer, an upholsterer. William Tite, who was elected MP for Bath in 1855, paid for wooden models of the two designs to be set up in Abbey Church Yard for a final decision to be made. It seemed that everyone agreed that the fountains looked out of scale in the Church Yard and the models were moved to the semi-circular space, occupied by a cab stand, at the east of Bath Street. This was thought to be a better location, and it was closer to the pumps in York Street that would supply it with mineral water. The Hot Water Committee chose the simpler of the two designs with the support of

The Abbey Church Yard, where the wooden models of the fountains were initially set up

Tite, who, as well as being the town's MP, was also a well-known architect who had rebuilt the Royal Exchange in London and designed many grand railway stations. Tite promised that he would send an architect from his own office to oversee the building of the fountain. A subscription list was opened to pay for the fountain, a quotation from Jesse Stamp for doing the work having already been accepted.[74]

By the middle of May, work had started on the foundations. The Hot Water Fountain Committee urged the builders to finish the work so that the fountain could be illuminated as part of the celebrations on 29 May to mark the end of the Crimean War, which had always been part of the plan.[75] Although they failed to meet the deadline, the fountain still played a role in the ceremony, with water from the mains supply running through it and the mayor and councillors processing from the abbey to inaugurate it.[76] A month later it was still not completed – although good progress was being made – and it was eventually finished in August.[77]

The Tite Mineral Water Fountain of 1856

The fountain had at its base a large circular basin, from the centre of which rose a 16-foot-square stone kiosk with four arched openings. On the top of this was a large flat vase, known as a tazza, which had been supplied by Pieroni, who, as we have seen, was well known for importing ornamental items from Italy. In the middle of the tazza was a stone urn from which flowed mineral water that filled the bowl before pouring over its rim into the lower basin. The *Bath Chronicle* noted that 'the red mouths of four lions in the middle of the column also pour forth their crystal and fiery streams behind the falling streams above.'[78] William Parker, who admired the fountain, wrote that

> the sight of the unusual work of nature and art excites the curious stranger to approach the reservoir with an eye of admiration and surprise; on putting their hand into this inimitable hot water a sudden drawback of the body is shown to the bystanders, who are a little amused at the shock of agreeableness to the novice.

Not unexpectedly, financial problems surrounded the construction of the fountain. By August the Hot Water Fountain Committee had not paid Jesse Stamp, the builder, for his work, and he instructed solicitors to sue them.[79] Before this was resolved, however, Stamp became insolvent and sold the debt at a discount to a solicitor called Bartrum. The committee did not have the money to pay Bartrum the balance of £55 12s 3d owed; and in 1857 Bartrum offered members of the committee the opportunity to pay him four pounds each from their own pockets, which was a reduction of six pounds from the amount actually owed. As an alternative, he offered to let someone he knew demolish the fountain and reclaim the materials in return for paying off the debt. Most of the committee members paid their four pounds. One of them, however, a watchmaker and jeweller in Stall Street called George Lansdown, refused to pay, claiming that he had always been against the fountain but had been 'outmanoeuvred ' by the committee. He said that, when the decision to proceed with the fountain was taken, he had argued it should be delayed until all the money to pay for it had been collected, but when the chairman told him he would pay for any shortfall if necessary, he acquiesced. James Williams denied that the chairman had made any such commitment and said that people were trying to 'burk' the committee. Bartrum took Lansdown to the county court where the latter was ordered to pay the full amount of £10 7s.

Lansdown took the opportunity, however, to voice his opinion that, 'from the day that Mr Tite had appeared in the Abbey Church Yard, the matter had assumed a political character.'[80] Tite was a Liberal, while Lansdown was a Tory who viewed the fountain as a piece of political propaganda for the Liberals. It was not only Conservatives who disliked it, however; even some of those who had instigated it disliked it. The chairman of the

AN ENTHUSIAST FOR THE TITE FOUNTAIN

William Parker, MRCS, LAC was a great supporter of the Hot Water Fountain, in contrast to the press and the public, who were overwhelmingly opposed to it. This was very much in line with his eccentric, obsessive, contrarian character. He had firm views on the science of physiology and delivered public lectures to promulgate them, but in 1856, having got no response or applause, decided to publish a pamphlet called *New Physiological Views with an Appendix on the Bath Thermal Waters.*[82] This was shortly after the fountain had been built, and for rhetorical effect he compared it with the recently-constructed Menai Tubular Bridge. The bridge, he declared, was much admired and painted by artists whereas the fountain was seen as an 'encumbrance and a nuisance'. He argued, however, that, in the way that the fountain brought together excellence in nature and artifice, the fountain was superior to the bridge. After all, he argued 'we can have another Menai Tubular Bridge etc. but another Bath Mineral Hot Water Fountain can nowhere else be seen'. Its uniqueness arose from the combination of the health-giving qualities of the mineral water and the beauty of the man-made fountain. Many Bathonians disliked the brown staining, caused by iron oxide in the water, that marred the fountain as soon as it was built, but for Parker it was a thing of beauty:

> *The natural colouring of the Bath Stone, by the mineral water cannot be surpassed by the [artist's] brush ... The Bath Mineral Hot Water Fountain is very analogous to the beauty and excellence of the English racing horses. The horse and the fountain are constituted of artificial and natural parts, that have caused a full display of excellence and beauty to the public. Both are endowed with natural colouring of exquisite tint, constituting external beauty. The excellence of the water and the fountain will shine forth as beautiful and praiseworthy as the winning horse.*

He was very concerned that the fountain should not be removed, as many wished it to be. His views had their origin in a peculiarly Victorian food fad. He believed that nitrogen was the major chemical element in people, food, explosives and manure; and therefore that foods high in nitrogen were nutritious and health giving. He asked why rum and brandy were unhealthy whereas tea, coffee, cocoa, Irish moss and asparagus were nutritious. The answer, he claimed, was that 'the blood and brain of man has the same constituents as tea, coffee, cocoa etc.'[83] Bath mineral water was also rich in nitrogen, hence his commitment to it. Although all this may seem eccentric today, the belief that the nitrogen of the spa waters was efficacious was not uncommon in the nineteenth century.[84]

City Act Committee said that the fountain was not built to the design he had approved. Even James Williams admitted that most people thought it unsightly and that the design had been changed after approval had been given. There had been a number of alterations to the plan, some caused by 'hydraulic problems' and some by the decision to build it not in the Abbey Church Yard (which was where Stamp had quoted for) but in Bath Street. The *Bath Chronicle* declared that the fountain was 'an abominable lump of deformity, stained with iron, looking like a heap of worn out marine stores, or something saved from a fire'.[81]

James Williams was redoubtable and did not give up on the possibility that the fountain could be remodelled and improved. In the autumn of 1858, when many were calling for its removal, he made such a proposal to Bath corporation.[85] When it was discussed at the Bath and Pump Room Committee it was said that the fountain was a discredit to the city, a receptacle for rubbish and dead cats and an encouragement for young boys to play havoc in the fountain's basin.[86] Most councillors, however, thought that the object of having a hot mineral water fountain as an advertisement for the city was a good one.

James Williams brought in Pieroni to help him redesign the fountain and they took their proposal to the City Act Committee, which decided that it would be better to improve rather than remove the fountain. Twenty-three residents of Bath Street, no doubt encouraged by Pieroni as one of the street's leading residents, supported Mr William's proposal. The plan was to remove all the features of the fountain that offended, including the basin at its foot, and to protect it with iron railings. However, Pieroni was away in London and it was decided to delay a decision until his return, when he and Williams could bring forward a detailed plan.[87] Before that happened, however, local interest transferred to the general election called for April 1859.

The 1859 Election and the Hot Water Fountain

Bath was represented by two members of parliament. Prior to the 1859 election they were Arthur Hallam Elton and William Tite, both Liberals. Tite stood again in the election of that year but Elton did not; according to some he had been unfairly manipulated by the Liberals into giving up his seat so that Thomas Phinn could stand. Phinn had been elected a Liberal MP for Bath in 1852 but resigned in 1855 to become Second Secretary to the Admiralty. Many Bath voters took his preference for a paid government post as a betrayal of the city's trust, although as a radical in favour of electoral reform many the working classes in the city still supported him. The Tory candidate was Arthur Way. Bath politics were dominated by the Liberals in the second half of the nineteenth century.

Busts of William Tite and Thomas Phinn still flank the entrance lobby of Bath's Guildhall. The bust of Tite (on the left) is by William Theed and was presented to the city in 1873. The bust of Phinn (on the right), by an unknown sculptor, was presented to the city in 1867.

The city was divided between the upper town, occupied by the gentry, the clergy, the military and the learned professions, whilst the lower town was the province of the commercial classes – tradesmen, shopkeepers and small property owners.[88] This latter group was larger and tended to vote Liberal in municipal and parliamentary elections. Both Pieroni and James Williams belonged to this latter group and, unsurprisingly, both joined the election committees of the Liberal candidates.[89]

The election campaign became personal as Phinn and Way criticised each other's characters.[90] Phinn, however, seems to have been thin-skinned. He objected to Way referring to him as 'Tom'. During a speech at the Guildhall Phinn was reported as saying:

> I met a voter in Monmouth street ... who told me that Mr Way had called upon him and solicited his vote, but he said, 'no, Sir, I am going to vote for Mr Tite and Mr Phinn'; upon which Mr Way said, 'oh! Tom Phinn you mean!' . Now I think that was a piece of great familiarity. I am called Tom Phinn here among my friends, and I am called Tom Phinn in the House of Commons: and I do not object because I am Tom Phinn. But then for a gentleman of etiquette and decorum to take that familiarity with one he does not know...[91]

Phinn's attitude made him a target for the local satirists. Tite was already a target because of his connection with the mineral water fountain, one political bill poster ironically claiming that he was 'well known in architectural circles for the beauties and adoption of his HOT WATER FOUNTAIN which he is slanderously reported to have stood godfather to'. As Phinn seems to have delivered a speech to his followers from the fountain, which was adjacent to the Liberal party office in York Street, the fountain was used to lampoon both Liberal candidates.[92] Among the more scathing attacks were the verses below, which appeared in the pages of the staunchly Tory *Bath Chronicle* on 28 April 1859.[93]

MR. PHINN ON THE FOUNTAIN.

TUESDAY, 26th April.

Years since, from Bath Street Fountain
(Proof of Tite's classic taste),
A scant supply of water
Ran dribblingly to waste.

But lo ! Tom Phinn ascends and speaks—
When louder far and free'r,
Down comes, at once, a copious flood
Of very sour small beer.

ANOTHER.
THE FOUNTAIN OF ELOQUENCE.

What's this ? so lumbering, dirty, dry,
This Tite's Hot Water Fountain !
Below—a crowd of ragged boys—
Above, Tom Fin just mounting.

Another speech ? how apt the place !
Sure by some wag suggested ;
For on a fitter pedestal,
No statue ever rested.

To idle Fountain—idle man,—
How certain the attraction !
Both wait the stream of patronage—
Both are of Bath extraction.

Heavy pretensions, dull and dry,
More clumsy too than tapering ;
Both rather stained, and both their works
Exhale in misty vapouring.

Both out of place—then wherefore here ?
There's only one solution—
For neither would be standing now
But for Tite's contribution.

Sadly, the poetical quality of Bath satire had declined since Anstey's eighteenth-century invective verse.[94] On election day, Tite was elected but Phinn lost to Way, receiving 1,198 votes to Way's 1,349. Pieroni did not have a vote, even though he had become a British subject in April 1858, so either this was too late for him to be put onto the electoral roll or the rental value of his home was less than the ten pounds needed for him to be enfranchised. Williams, who had a house on Lyncombe Hill, did vote, giving one of his two votes to Tite and the other to Phinn.[95]

WAYSIDE WORDS.

MR. COOKHEM has the honour, as we hear, to announce to the BATH BOYS that he will show them the "WAY to the Poll" on Thursday, in the Orange Market.

MR. COOKHEM will let them see also two other would-be Representative Men, one of whom they knew before as the Man who, when he last was at the head of the Poll, FOUND HIS HAT TOO *TIGHT* FOR THE POLL OF HIS HEAD, and was well laughed at for crossing the gangway of the House of Columns, as he will be now for crossing another *WAY*, if he doesn't mind.

The same Gentleman is well known in Architectural Circles for the beauty and adaptation of his HOT WATER FOUNTAIN, which he is slanderously reported to have stood Godfather to. Report further says that after the next Reform Bill he is likely to stand for Wincanton out of compliment to his Friend Commissioner Yeh, whose system of Heads and Tails he particularly approves, as compared with the atrocities of the unpopular English Minister.

The other Orange Favourite is the great PROTEGE of the Russian Court for the patient-service he LIBERALLY rendered the Enemies of England during the late war. He may be called indeed the Czar's Candidate. He is generally acknowledged to be one of the most promising young men in the County. He promised victory to Russia, and disgrace and failure to England, and now he promises to be a good Member for Waterborough, if we'll let him; but we mean to leave him behind a long way, dont we, Boys? That is, if the PLUMPERS do their duty, and the Split Peas don't get too Cheap.

T. stands for a Tailor of Tooley Street,
Dear friend of Commissioner YEH:
And F. stands for history's F'ELTON,
Who'd stab England if PAM were away:
But W. stands for the name of a man
Whom F'ELTON and Tailors may beat if they can.

A broadsheet from the 1859 election

The Pieroni and Williams Fountain

It is not surprising that soon after the election Williams and Pieroni presented their plans for redesigning the fountain that had caused the Liberals so much embarrassment. There were three committees whose approval was necessary if the changes to the fountain were to be made. They were the Hot Water Fountain Committee, the Baths and Pump Room Committee and the City Act Committee. Pieroni and Williams took their plans to the Fountain Committee on 16 May, and they were approved subject to a report being made to the Act Committee. This was done and the proposals were again approved. The Baths and Pump Room Committee, who also gave their assent on 26 May, were more concerned with the engineering issues of supplying the hot mineral water to the fountain than with the aesthetics of the design, and Mr Stothert, a member of the committee, was appointed to review the capacity and fitness of the proposed hydraulics.[96]

Williams focussed on the engineering of the fountain, while Pieroni was responsible for the design. He proposed to remove the lions and the large tazza, and place a statue of Bladud on the kiosk. This was an interesting choice. The story of Bladud as the founder of the city of Bath had been largely accepted as true in the eighteenth century, and was much publicised by John Wood, the architect. By the nineteenth century, however, its status as a myth had been accepted, and it was considered that Bath should base its antiquity on the rediscovered Roman temple and baths rather than on a fairy story. However, there was a revival of interest in the Bladud story in the middle of the century, with one historian claiming that 'a touch of myth sets off a strong history as a waif of cloud is a graceful accompaniment to the sides of a mountain.'[97] Bath's tourism industry was in decline and the city council were concerned to reverse the trend. The supporters of the mineral water fountain clearly saw it as a tourist attraction, and perhaps one whose attractiveness could be enhanced by association with the figure of Bladud. Another part of the city's plan to boost visitors was to replace the White Hart Inn adjacent to the fountain with the Grand Pump Room Hotel, which eventually opened in 1869.[98] The choice of Bladud was still a risky one if people remembered the satirical fountain design of 1855, even though Pieroni's Bladud was dressed as a swineherd rather than appearing naked. Bladud was not the only new adornment to the fountain. Around its base were to be four figures representing the seasons. Instead of flowing over and around the central kiosk the mineral water would flow down from within it, and the source and direction of the flow would be changed from time to time to maintain interest. Finally, to prevent boys jumping in the water and splashing the public, the whole fountain was to be surrounded by an iron railing.

The Grand Pump Room Hotel, which can be seen beyond the colonnade, opened in 1869 as part of the city's bid to atract visitors.

When work started on remodelling the fountain in November 1859, Williams wrote to the Baths and Pump Room Committee for permission to attach pumps to the existing steam engine in York Street. The pumps would take water from the Queens Bath, but would be arranged so as not to deprive the Private Baths of the volume of water that they needed. In exchange, Williams agreed to repair the steam engine at no cost. He also asked for permission to apply to the public for subscriptions to defray the anticipated cost of £200 to complete the work on the fountain.[99] The omens were good for a favourable reception of the new fountain. In November 1859, the *Bath and Cheltenham Gazette* declared that, although they had to reserve judgement, as hoardings were still up around the fountain, 'we feel strongly disposed towards a favourable verdict'. They also noted that, as well as designing the fountain, Pieroni was superintending the building work and was responsible for a great proportion of the cost.[100]

By 8 December, the hoardings had been taken down, and one newspaper reported that the fountain

> presents an attractive appearance that contrasts very favourably with the unsightly object which previously occupied the site; and execution of the work reflects great credit on Mr J Williams and Signor Pieroni, by whose enterprise and public spirit it has been called into being.[101]

A correspondent in the *Bath Chronicle* agreed:

> Touching the Bladud fountain ... the present one is a great improvement on the rusty candlestick, which our worthy member [of parliament] had designed to lighten the darkness of those who were ignorant of the virtues of Bath water. [102]

However, a letter from 'A Bathonian' in the *Bath Journal* pointed out that the hydraulics had not been finished, and the supply 'of hot water with a cloud of steam [that] may be calculated upon throughout the greatest portion of each day' could only be anticipated.[103] The anonymous correspondent also called for readers to subscribe to the cost of the fountain. The inclusion in the same newspaper of an advertisement from Pieroni seeking subscriptions for the fountain suggests that he may have written the letter. He certainly cashed in on the publicity

The Bladud Fountain of 1859 by Pieroni and Williams

The full text of the letter from 'A Bathonian' – possibly Pieroni himself – which appeared in the *Bath Journal* on 9 December 1859:

I think the citizens of Bath are much indebted to Signor Pieroni for his spirited success in erecting, at his own risk, the present pretty and complete fountain in Bath Street. The contrast with the former is so marked that all are bound to admire it. The chief object of admiration is the surmounted figure representing the discarded leper, in the occupation of a swineherd – discovering the hot waters, the wonders of which are well known throughout the length and breadth of the land. Who knows but that the structure stands over the very spot where the outcast first set eyes on the congenial stream, for here is the very centre of the flowing springs. I think the pensive mien, the dejected attitude and the kind of melancholy expression of the figure are happy ideas considering the nature of the subject. The princely but discarded leper – the leprous swineherd with his leprous swine, afterwards the great King Bladud.

Thanks to the promoters of such an idea, calculated as it is to perpetuate the history of such an event – an event to which Bath owes its origin, and which has contributed more to the luxuries of the inhabitants through the ages than any other thing connected to this ancient city ... What an advertisement to the baths! Verily I think that the Corporation might with consistency vote the cost of the erection, but that the City of Bath Act prevents it let us then as citizens take care that the designer and builder be not a loser. Let us care and keep up the spirit of reviving our ancient, but not yet 'grass grown' city as shown by one or two individuals in this and some other generous and patriotic accomplishments, and Bath will soon become the observed and the admired of all travellers, but we must substantially support the promoters who so nobly gave their time, talents and moneys for the improvements which they with so much difficulty carry out.

A Bathonian

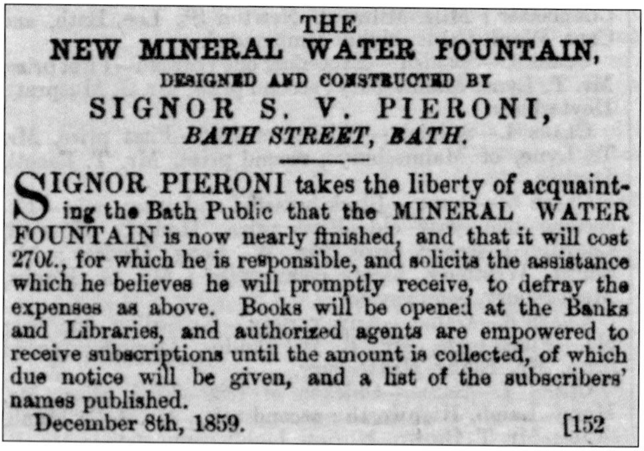

THE
NEW MINERAL WATER FOUNTAIN,
DESIGNED AND CONSTRUCTED BY
SIGNOR S. V. PIERONI,
BATH STREET, BATH.

SIGNOR PIERONI takes the liberty of acquainting the Bath Public that the MINERAL WATER FOUNTAIN is now nearly finished, and that it will cost 270*l.*, for which he is responsible, and solicits the assistance which he believes he will promptly receive, to defray the expenses as above. Books will be opened at the Banks and Libraries, and authorized agents are empowered to receive subscriptions until the amount is collected, of which due notice will be given, and a list of the subscribers' names published.

December 8th, 1859. [152

Pieroni's appeal for subscriptions

surrounding the fountain – and the proximity of Christmas – by announcing in the *Bath Chronicle* and the *Bath Journal* that he had 'just received direct from Italy an assortment of marble and alabaster ornamental goods suitable for Christmas presents and respectfully solicits an early inspection'.[104] As we shall see, importing art objects from Italy was another aspect of Pieroni's business.

The first call for subscriptions to pay for the fountain was not entirely successful. Although 198 people subscribed, only £80 was raised, leaving a shortfall of £190. Some notable figures contributed, including the mayor, Dr Randle Wilbraham Falconer, who was also senior physician at the Mineral Water Hospital, and James Tunstall, a doctor and author of *Rambles about Bath*. William Tite, MP, must have been unconcerned that the original fountain that he had championed had been replaced, because he donated the second largest amount of five pounds to the subscription list. Most of the contributions, however, were for less than a pound and came from the tradesmen of the lower town. The nobility and gentry of the upper town largely failed to subscribe. So, in May 1860, Pieroni printed and distributed an eight-page appeal to the 'Nobility, Gentry and Citizens of Bath' for more money.[105] The appeal included the legend of Bladud and lauded 'the true artistic representation of the supposed founder of the City of Bath, and discoverer of the medicinal virtues of the hot mineral water therein'. The pamphlet concluded:

> As Messrs Signor PIERONI and J WILLIAMS embarked in this undertaking purely in the spirit of the *public good*, thinking that one of the most remarkable phenomenon in the world; the original soul, and the present wonder of the City, should not be so unobserved as heretofore, but be more publicly displayed within the very locality of

> its discovery! It is hoped the public generally will see fit to prevent their suffering a *pecuniary* loss, as well as a large amount of time which they have cheerfully given to the public gratification.

Although they hoped that people would not be 'backward in coming forward', it seems unlikely that this second appeal would have made up such a large shortfall. Williams, who ran a thriving engineering business, however, may have been in a better position to absorb any loss than Pieroni, who, as has been seen, was in financial trouble by 1863.

The fountain may have been finished, but it suffered the same hydraulic problems as the previous one. It seems that by July 1860 hot mineral water was still not flowing through it. James Williams tendered to replace the boiler of the York Street steam engine and was also given permission to attach the pipe feeding the fountain directly to the pipe supplying the Private Baths rather than taking water from the Queen's Bath as originally proposed.[106] By 1861 the steam engine was doing its job and delivering the mineral water to the fountain, although never as efficiently and as continuously as had been hoped. Perhaps the engine was unreliable and this may have been why Pieroni got to know James Beer, the engineer, well. A few years later Beer got into a brawl in York Street with Henry Fowler. The two men were in dispute over the finances of the United Provident Society and, on seeing Beer, Fowler exclaimed 'thee was pointing at I', which started an argument and led to a fight. The two men charged and counter charged each other with assault. Pieroni stood as a witness for Beer, who was found not guilty.[107]

Once working the fountain had its critics. One, calling himself Civis, wrote to the newspaper to protest

> against the hideous perpetration just erected opposite the Baths. The head and body of a large man on a child's legs, grasping a big stick and mounted on a double arch, with four misformed applewomen at the four corners, is surely no fit indication of the present prevailing taste and knowledge of art in a city 'whose architecture' says Macaulay 'must delight the eye accustomed to the masterpieces of Vitruvius and Palladio'; and in a place always remarkable for the eminence of its medical men ... the public exhibition of these outrageous instances of malformation and false anatomy must be felt as a libel by every member of the profession.[108]

Whether the figure of Bladud was malformed can be judged from the photographs on pages 34 and 35. Certainly, others disagreed with Civis and thought the new fountain, as has been seen, 'a great improvement'. This ambivalence towards the fountain continues to the present day and its varying reputation, even as it went through many transformations, reflects the struggle Pieroni had in stabilising his own position within Bath society.

5

PUBLICAN AND ART DEALER

Pieroni's business was not limited to selling his own work. He also became a pub landlord and imported all kinds of Italian art works.

The Eagle Hotel

In 1851, No 4 Bath Street was in multiple occupation and Stefano and Rebekah Pieroni were sharing it with several other families. Ten years later, they had it to themselves. Their nephew, Martin Pieroni, had moved from London to live with them, and they also employed a young servant called Lewis Ellen.[109] We have already seen that, when Pieroni was nearly bankrupt in 1863, he described himself as a wine merchant as well as a modeller. His ambition was to run a public house at 4 Bath Street, although when it opened he referred to it, with a typical dash of grandeur, as a hotel.

He first opened a beerhouse at no. 4 in the early 1860s. The 1830 Beerhouse Act enabled anyone to brew and sell beer if they could afford two guineas for a licence. The act was designed to wean the public away from the evils of gin and other hard liquor and onto beer, which was seen as a more virtuous drink. One consequence of the act was that local magistrates did not have the same veto over beerhouse licences as they had over full licences. Pieroni applied for, but was denied, a full licence on several occasions.[110] He nevertheless tried to obtain a better class of customer by letting out his large drawing room, 'beautifully decorated and with every convenience', for lectures, private balls and parties.[111] Having been denied a joint spirit and billiards licence in August 1867, Pieroni tried, the following month, to obtain a licence for billiards alone. This application, however, was adjourned due to a legal wrangle over whether sufficient notice had been given for such an appeal.[112] In October 1867, John Mitchell applied to transfer the licence of the White Hart Tap to Pieroni's house, as the Tap was being demolished to make room for the Grand Pump Room Hotel. Although Mitchell undertook to be Pieroni's tenant and run the pub for him, the magistrates obviously thought this a ruse by Pieroni after his 'ineffectual' earlier bid for a licence, and refused the transfer.[113] In August the following year Pieroni made yet another application for a spirit and billiards licence. He had worked hard at this application, which he employed a lawyer to advocate, and gathered a great deal of support for.

It was reported that 'the house is a very respectable one. Pieroni speaks several languages and his house is frequented by foreigners.'[114] As always, the Bath Temperance Association objected. However, a petition from all the residents of Bath Street in favour of the application was presented. It was also pointed out that there were no other licensed houses in the street, that Pieroni had a room very handsomely fitted up for billiards, and that there were few such others in the city. The application was approved.

No. 4 Bath Street became the Eagle Hotel, which Pieroni emblazoned with a plaster cast of a spread-eagle above the colonnade.[115] Working for Pieroni in the hotel in 1871 were his 19-year-old niece, Maria Pieroni, as a barmaid, and Louis Dal Toso from Venice, as a waiter.[116] Martin Pieroni, Maria's brother, was still there as well, working as an upholsterer, and another upholsterer, called Augusto Pizzie, was a lodger. As he was the only lodger, the Eagle was clearly more of a pub than a hotel.

No photographs of No 4 Bath Street during Pieroni's tenancy seem to have survived. The spread-eagle he placed above the colonnade also escaped the attention of photographers, even though it remained on the building until comparitively recently. On the Edwardian postcard above, it can just be glimpsed to the left of the fountain. The most detailed record we have of it, however, is the sketch on the left by Cyril Beazer, which he made in 1963, shortly before carrying out work on the south side of Bath Street, which entailed the eagle's removal. Its fate and current whereabouts are unknown.

In 1869, a year after Pieroni became a fully-licensed victualler, he found himself in trouble for having three unstamped measures for selling spirits. The measures were correct but they had not been checked and stamped by the Weights and Measures Office. Pieroni's excuse was that the Weights and Measures Office was only open twice a week and he had not had the opportunity to get his newly-bought measures checked. He was fined a nominal sum of sixpence per measure. As a licensed victualler, Pieroni joined the Licensed Victuallers' Association, and, when they sent a petition to the mayor and magistrates of Bath in 1873, he was one of the signatories. The new mayor claimed to have consulted with the 'most respectable inn and hotel keepers' in the city and come to the view that they agreed that 11pm was a suitable closing time for pubs. But the Licensed Victuallers Association argued that they should also have been consulted.[117] The mayor accepted that 11pm was not favoured by the victuallers but still thought it was best for the order and tranquillity of the city.

Among the stock Pieroni imported for the Eagle was a quart of brandy from the *Thomas Powell* from Charente, which docked in Bristol in October 1870.[118] In July 1875 came a larger consignment of four casks of wine from Charente.[119] A few months later, in October 1875, he transferred the licence of the Eagle to George Ley, who ran it for six years before transferring it to William Walton in 1881.[120]

Importer of Italian Art

Pieroni seems to have visited Italy on a number of occasions to collect sculpture, ornaments and paintings that he could retail in Britain. In October 1858, he advertised that he had just returned from Italy and he was selling 'a choice collection of beautifully executed alabaster and marble works' at sale rooms in Exeter.[121] A few months later, in January 1859, he announced that he was selling his imports at an auction house in Wine Street, Bristol:

> Signor Pieroni informs the nobility, gentry and the public of Bristol and Clifton that he has just received by the barque Camoglino direct from the workshops of Italy a large and well selected assortment of BEAUTIFUL WORKS OF ART in marble and alabaster suited to the most refined tastes … Signor Pieroni having made a personal selection of these excellent works can confidently invite all those who have a taste for refinement to their inspection.[122]

He added that 'a large quantity of paintings by the Italian masters' was 'on sale at 4 Bath Street, Bath'. He ventured as far afield as Worcester, where he instructed an auctioneer to sell a 'collection of magnificent Italian sculptures imported directly from Leghorn'.[123] These copies of 'the celebrated works in the galleries and academies of Rome, Florence and Naples' including statues of 'The Amazons', 'The Graces', 'Cupid and Psyche', 'The Four Dancing Girls', 'Venus Rising from the Waves', and 'The Flight into Egypt'. Smaller ornamental items included vases and ewers (from eight inches to six feet tall), fruit baskets, paperweights, ink stands and 'other tasteful articles'.

In 1862 Morris & Sons' auction house in Bath held a sale of 25 cases of Italian statuary imported from Florence,

> by an agent who has availed himself of the unparalleled depression of trade attendant on the recent political struggles in that country to secure some of the choicest specimens of artistic skill ever imported into England.[124]

The agent is not named but from the tone of the advertisement and the type of stock imported it was probably Pieroni. After his near bankruptcy in 1863, Pieroni had to clear his stock to stay in business and in 1864 and 1865 he put a large collection of sculptures, statuary, garden vases, gold and bronze brackets, bas reliefs, marble tazzas, plaster figures, bronzes and marble mantelpieces up for auction without reserve.[125]

Pieroni continued to sell artworks imported from Italy at auction. Some of the items offered in a sale at George Trick's auction rooms in Bristol in 1880 seem to have been funerary pieces: they included ten-and-a-half-foot obelisks topped with crosses, an angel representing the Last Judgement and a brother and sister weeping over their parents' graves.[126] In 1885, he placed an advertisement in the *Bath Chronicle* to

> inform the public that he has returned from Italy and has succeeded in bringing with him a rare assortment of old, original and valuable OIL PAINTINGS executed by some of the best masters, consisting of two battle pieces representing the engagement at Lepanto, two beautiful figures by Ambale Caraic, a fine and original painting by Sarvatore Rosa and several others.[127]

The newspaper compositor was obviously unfamiliar with Italian art history: the two misnamed painters are Annibale Carracci (1560-1609) and Salvator Rosa (1615-1673). Whether the paintings advertised were genuine old masters or copies is an intriguing question that will be returned to later.

6

WORTHY CITIZEN OR SOCIAL CLIMBER AND SWAGGERER?

Stefano Pieroni's position in Bath society was liminal. He was on or near several thresholds. He was from a labouring, itinerant background seeking to establish himself in the city's municipal and commercial class. He was a proud Italian but loyal to Britain and its Queen. He was an artisan who was aspiring to be an artist, and frequently referred to himself as such. As we shall see, in attempting to cross these thresholds his acts of good citizenship were accompanied by a swagger that could lead him to exaggerate his achievements and to claim sole credit for things that others had had a hand in. He needed the trust of others to achieve his ambitions and, when his trust was not reciprocated, he became disputatious and litigious. Such behaviour would have raised his public profile, and he may consciously have sought to distinguish himself as a 'character' – a stereotypical Italian – in middle-class Bath society.

Civic Good Works

The inauguration of the mineral water fountain in 1859 gave a massive boost to Pieroni's bid to achieve respectability in the city, and led to him being involved in plans for improving Royal Victoria Park. There was a general feeling that the lack of statuary in Bath's public places reflected badly on its status as a tourist destination. Pieroni, along with Thomas Corbould, the landlord of the Lamb Brewery in Stall Street, came up with a solution. They had bought from a Mr Brewer of Box a collection of stone vases and an eight-foot-high statue of the Goddess of Sculpture. The statue had been made by John Osborne, a local self-taught sculptor, around 1835, since when it had been lying, unregarded, in Brewer's yard. Osborne had also made the colossal head of Jupiter that can still be seen today in the Great Dell in Royal Victoria Park. Among the other items acquired from Mr Brewer was the tazza that had been on top of Tite's mineral water fountain until Pieroni had it removed.

Pieroni and Corbould offered the collection to the city on condition that it be 'erected in a place of public resort'.[128] Royal Victoria Park

Opposite: Osborne's bust of Jupiter around 1910. Although it still stands in the Great Dell today, the plinth is no longer covered in ivy.

was the obvious choice. Others became involved in this act of civic philanthropy: James Wilson, the architect, designed the massive stone pedestals that the vases and statue were to stand on; James Maggs of Princes Buildings, a local painter of portraits, animals and old Bath scenes, drew the collection of vases and statuary in an imaginary setting; and William Lewis of Union Street prepared and exhibited a lithograph of the work. Alderman William Bush of the Circus paid for the work to be done, and the tazza, which can still be seen today, was erected in May 1861.[129] In July, when all the vases and statuary had been erected, the *Bath Chronicle* declared that they 'reflect the highest credit on the taste and liberality of those who promoted the object'.[130] Unfortunately, Thomas Corbould had died in April, aged 43, before he could hear this praise. The statue of the Goddess of Sculpture has since disappeared.

Donating the statuary put Pieroni alongside other notables in the city. Providing statuary for the adornment of city festivities had been for some time a standard tactic in Pieroni's efforts towards achieving local celebrity. When the Bath and West Show was held in Bath in 1854, a triumphal arch was erected at the entrance to Union Street, with two full-size figures of Spring and Summer from the studio of Signor Pieroni, on either side.[131] When a Citizens' Ball was held at the Assembly Rooms in 1860, 'under the patronage of the mayor and Mr Tite, MP', Pieroni's house in Bath Street was one of the places where tickets could be obtained.

In 1861, when a banquet was held at the Guildhall in honour of the mayor, Mr Murch, Pieroni contributed vases and statues to decorate the Banqueting Room.[132] When he provided statues to ornament the Assembly Rooms for the Bath and County Club Ball in 1872, the *Western Daily Press* reported that the venue

> had been decorated at considerable expense, and what with the embellishments of the upholsterer, the florist, the statuary and the painter the suite of apartments presented a luxurious and tasteful appearance.[133]

Floral fetes were also regular features of the Bath social scene. They were held in Sydney Gardens, and, as well as displays of plants, flowers and other produce, featured band concerts and other entertainments.[134] They were organised by the Bath Royal United Horticultural Society until 1855, when the Hanoverian Band Committee took them over. In 1857, Pieroni and Maggs decorated the gardens for the fete. Around the serpentine walk were pedestals supporting handsome vases supplied by Pieroni, while on higher ground, also supplied by Pieroni, was

> a massive pedestal, with angular buttresses curving gracefully outwards, and terminating in four pedestals supporting vases. Upon the structure was placed a dwarf column with a group of figures representing Flora

Osborne's statue of the Goddess of Sculpture surrounded by various plinths and vases, including Pieroni's tazza, in 1855. This lithograph, from a painting by JC Maggs, was part of a publicity campaign to have the group of scupltures erected in Royal Victoria Park.

A view of the tazza in Royal Victoria Park in the 1920s, when Pieroni's name was still clearly legible

> encouraging her votaries. The Goddess was presented with a wreath of flowers on her head and her arms extended.[135]

Maggs and Pieroni provided a similar display the following year.[136]

In September 1860, the second fete of the season was held in Sydney Gardens. Once again Pieroni placed statuary along the principal walks and avenues.[137] Unfortunately the weather was inclement and marquees had to be erected to house the exhibits, which included wax and paper flowers alongside real ones. The *Bath Chronicle* noted that

> the committee has very much increased the material attractions of the gardens by the display at different points of a number of gaily coloured banners and ... engaged Signor Pieroni of Bath Street to decorate the grounds with statuary, a duty which he has discharged, not only to the satisfaction of the committee, but also to that of the visitors who appeared to be very much pleased with the effect.[138]

It added that the music was good and the gardens had 'been frequented by the most brilliant and fashionable assemblages'. Not everyone was happy, however; the report mentioned that some exhibitors had not acquiesced in the judges' decisions – perhaps a characteristic of all flower shows.[139]

Pieroni also enhanced his position in civic life by subscribing to various good causes. He bought ten shillings worth of shares in the Theatre Royal, he contributed half a crown to the memorial fund for the Prince Consort in 1862, and in 1859 he gave 10s 6d to the fund to commission a bust of the mayor, Dr Falconer. Perhaps he was hoping to get the commission for the bust, which went instead to his competitor Louis Gardie. Gardie's bust, which was much admired, can still be seen in the Mineral Water Hospital. Pieroni was not unusual in making these contributions. Mrs Corbould, who had taken over as landlady of the Lamb Brewery when her husband died, also contributed to these subscription lists.

Pieroni's Business Circles and Relationships

Business in Victorian Bath for people like Pieroni meant having a circle of friends and acquaintances, such as the Corboulds, through whom, and with whom, work could be obtained. Bonds of reciprocity and mutual obligation were essential, although these sometimes broke down and the parties found themselves in court. Business seldom ran smoothly for Pieroni and he was often engaged in litigious disputes.

Sometimes this was because he was too trusting. In 1864, he was working for Searle, the builder of Bridgwater Town Hall.[140] Pieroni was responsible for the plasterwork, which he sent to Bridgwater by the Great Western Railway (GWR). There were no problems until the final consignment was 'entrusted to the haulier' in November. It never arrived, and Pieroni sued the GWR for the cost of the consignment, £7 10s, plus a further £13 13s

2d. This was to cover the cost not only of making new plaster fittings, but also of travelling to Bridgwater and making new moulds, as he had broken the originals after the final consignment had been despatched. The lawyers for the GWR argued that, as Searle had agreed to pay for transporting the goods, they became his property as soon as they were delivered to the station in Bath. The subsequent loss, therefore, was Searle's and not Pieroni's. Further, they argued, there was no clause in the contract between Searle and Pieroni requiring delivery of the goods to Bridgwater. Therefore Pieroni had not been obliged to redo the work that had been lost. The judge found for the GWR, who agreed not to press for costs if Searle would agree not to sue the GWR. This meant that, even though the GWR paid no compensation, Searle received the new plasterwork, and the only loser was Pieroni.

On occasion it was his customers that caused Pieroni problems. In 1864, a Mrs Blane of Great Pulteney Street discussed with Pieroni making a memorial to her son, who had died in India, to be erected in the chapel in Queen Square. Pieroni went ahead and spent seven pounds on a marble tablet for the memorial, but Mrs Blane changed her mind and said she did not want the memorial. When he took her to court, the lawyers made long speeches about what counts as a legal contract, as a result of which the jury decided that Pieroni had 'acted on reasonable grounds but was mistaken as to his having really received an order'.[141] He lost the case.

Sometimes it was the trust he placed in his colleagues that was misplaced. In the spring of 1865, he became friends with a portrait painter called Vichery. Pieroni told Vichery that he had a client who wanted a portrait of an Italian called Vito. However the client did not want to engage an inferior artist, so it was suggested that Vichery paint a portrait of Pieroni first, to convince the client of the quality of Vichery's work. In this way, Vichery would get the Vito commission and, in return for his portrait, Pieroni would make a bust of Vichery. Pieroni would also get a share of the profit from Vito's portrait and a 10% commission on other work Vichery obtained through him. Pieroni also lent him £2 10s and bought him six shillings worth of beer.

Then Vichery announced that he was about to leave Bath. When Pieroni pressed him to settle his accounts, he refused to pay either the commission or the fifteen shillings for the bust. As a result of their discussion, however, Pieroni, who seems to have been completely hoodwinked, paid Vichery a further pound to finish his portrait. When no portrait was forthcoming, Pieroni took him to court. Vichery admitted that Pieroni had lent him money and bought him beer, but denied that he had received a commission for Vito's portrait. He also claimed to have completed the portrait of Pieroni, who now owed him twenty-five guineas for it. The case shows the complex transactions that could be involved in everyday business. On this occasion, the judge found for Pieroni and awarded him the £10 14s he was claiming.[142]

Disputes about commissions seem to have commonplace. In 1867, Pieroni became involved in a dispute between Mr Hill and Louis Gardie over the bust of Captain Speke discussed earlier. Hill had received a commission from Mr Fuller of Neston Park for a bust of Speke, whom he described as 'a distinguished relative', and engaged Gardie to make it. Gardie told him that, if the bust was a trade commission he would charge thirty-five guineas, but if he did it for the family he would charge fifty guineas. Hill told Gardie to deal directly with the family, and agreed that, instead of receiving the difference between thirty-five and fifty guineas as a middleman, he would charge Gardie 10% commission and 5% expenses. When Gardie completed the initial plaster model, most of the family approved it but one of them declared it was too large. As a result, Gardie kept the model for himself and received no payment. He was then commissioned by the dissenting family member, W Speke, to make a smaller bust in bronze for the family, for which a price of fifty guineas was agreed. Gardie saw this as a separate contract, not subject to his agreement with Hill, and did not pay him any commission. When Hill took Gardie to court for his share of the fifty guineas, Hill's lawyer argued that, as the scale of the bust was not Gardie's fault, Gardie was under no obligation to make a second bust. Consequently, the original contract still held, and commission was due. Hill asked Pieroni and several others to attest that it was common practice within the trade in Bath to pay commissions. Reeves, a sculptor, and Beckett, an upholsterer, testified to this, but Pieroni was more cautious and did not entirely corroborate Hill's claim.[143] This was odd, because he himself had previously won a court case for the payment of commission. It is also unlikely that Pieroni regarded Gardie favourably after he had done his best to prevent Pieroni from selling his bust of Speke. Moreover, Gardie and Pieroni would almost certainly have been political enemies: Gardie was a Bonapartist and Pieroni came from Lucca, a city that Napoleon had conquered and where he had installed his sister as duchess. Perhaps Pieroni was more annoyed with Hill for not giving him the commission to make the Speke bust in the first place than he was aggrieved at Gardie. But this can only be speculation.

Sometimes Pieroni resorted to the law to try to gain what seems like unfair benefit. Among the creditors with whom he came to an arrangement when he was insolvent in 1863 was a carpenter called Line. It appears that Pieroni had paid Line a greater proportion of the debt he owed him than the percentage agreed in the deed of composition, and took him to court in an attempt to claw back what he obviously considered excess payment. Unsurprisingly, the judge threw the claim out.[144]

Pieroni as Showman

Much of Pieroni's work was done in conjunction with others, but it seems that he sometimes claimed sole credit for such collaborative enterprises. The mineral water fountain was the result of the efforts of James Williams as well as of Pieroni. The copyright and workmanship of the bust of Speke, which he claimed as his own, were uncertain. He also allowed people to believe that he was a stone carver. Some thought that the mineral water fountain and the tazza in Royal Victoria Park had been 'carved with his own hand'.[145] Pieroni had been trained in modelling and plaster moulding and cannot have had any opportunity to learn to be a stone carver. Indeed, the tazza and other statuary were generally described as being 'from the studio of Signor Pieroni'.

There is one instance when Pieroni clearly made exaggerated claims. In May 1875, he advertised an exhibition of 'the Grand Oil Painting of Marsyas by Francesco Barbieri' at Houghton's Showrooms, Park Street Viaduct, Bristol. The following year, the same picture, now more accurately described as 'Apollo flaying Marsyas', was on display at the Drawbridge Skating Rink in Bristol. Admission was sixpence with a further sixpence for the hire of skates.

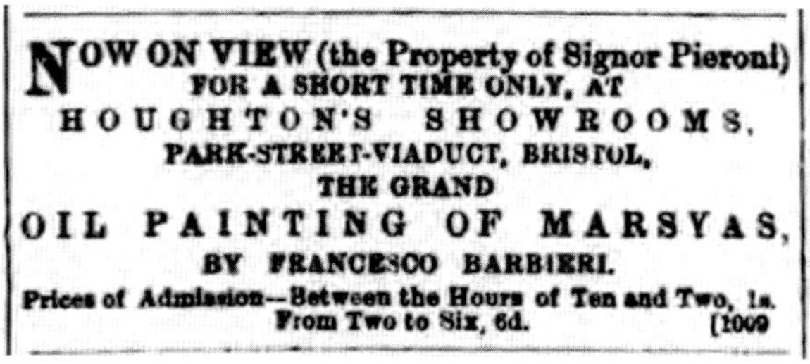
NOW ON VIEW (the Property of Signor Pieroni)
FOR A SHORT TIME ONLY, AT
HOUGHTON'S SHOWROOMS,
PARK-STREET-VIADUCT, BRISTOL,
THE GRAND
OIL PAINTING OF MARSYAS,
BY FRANCESCO BARBIERI.
Prices of Admission—Between the Hours of Ten and Two, 1s.
From Two to Six, 6d. [1009

An advertisement in the *Bristol Mercury* on 1 May 1878

At fourteen feet by twelve, the picture was certainly large, and the subject was gruesome enough to attract prurient interest. It was based on the story of a satyr – a creature with the hind quarters of a goat – who wagered Apollo that he could beat him in a musical contest. The winner could do whatever he wished with the loser. Not surprisingly, as he was a God, Apollo won and chose to flay Marsyas alive. The painting was by Francesco Barbieri (1591 -1666), better known by his nickname of Guercino, an important Italian Baroque artist.

The painting exhibited by Pieroni can only have been a copy, or at best 'from the studio of Guercino', because in 1828 the original was in the Palazzo Pitti in Florence, where it still is today. The original is also only around half the size of the one displayed in Bristol. Where Pieroni could have obtained such a painting is an interesting question.

Guercino's *Flaying of Marsyas by Apollo*

He could have bought it on one of his trips to Italy, although most of these took place after 1875 when he had ceased being a pub landlord. It is also possible he acquired it from Louis Gardie. When Gardie retired in 1868, he held an exhibition at the Assembly Rooms of both his own work and the collection of paintings and drawings he had built up over 46 years.[146] Among works by Correggio, Vandyke, Rubens, Poussin, Reynolds, Gainsborough, Watteau and Barker of Bath, the collection included a work by Gurchino (sic), which Pieroni may have purchased. Although this sounds like a fabulous collection, it is likely that most of the paintings were copies. Matters of artistic attribution were less important in provincial cities in Victorian times, and so perhaps Pieroni was not being deliberately sly, but simply unquestioning, in claiming his picture as an original.

Pieroni as Patriot

Stefano Pieroni's loyalties to both Italy and Britain can be seen in his responses to the issues of Italian unification and the call for a British volunteer force. In the 1840s and 1850s Italy was a geographical and cultural concept and not a political one. When Pieroni emigrated to Britain in 1837, he did so on an Austrian passport because he came from the Duchy of Lucca, then part of the Austrian empire. In the revolutionary turmoil in Europe in 1848, the Lombards forced the Austrian army under Radetsky to withdraw from Milan. When the news reached Tuscany, volunteer battalions were formed to join in the battle against the Austrians. One of the battalions was made up of university students; another, the *battaglione Luchese*, consisted of volunteers from Lucca, one of whom was Sergeant-Major Stefano Pieroni.[147] Could this be Stefano Vallerio Pieroni? We do not know his precise whereabouts in 1848: this was around the time he moved from London to Bath, but there is a possibility he was at home in Italy when the troubles broke out and volunteered to join the nationalist movement. His lack of military experience would not have ruled him out from being awarded the relatively high rank of Sergeant-Major: the Tuscan battalions were full of young enthusiasts, and commissions were awarded on the basis of enthusiasm rather than competence or experience. The Tuscan forces engaged with Radetsky at the battle of Curtatone on 29 May 1848, losing the battle nobly but giving the Piedmontese army time to position itself strategically against the Austrians. On balance, it seems unlikely that it was the Stefano Pieroni who came to Bath who fought against the Austrians, as Stefano Pieroni was not an uncommon name. Whether he was there, or not, however, his commitment to Italian reunification cannot be doubted.

Twelve years later, in 1860, the movement towards reunification had gathered momentum. Giuseppe Garibaldi assembled his force, known as 'the Thousand', and sailed to Sicily, then part of the Kingdom of the Two Sicilies ruled by Bourbon monarchs, with the aim of claiming it as part of the new Italy under the King of Sardinia. He landed on the island in May and his adventures were a European sensation. In June Pieroni joined with Signor Corrado, a teacher of Italian in Bath, to try to form a committee and raise subscriptions to support Garibaldi. Corrado delivered two lectures at the Assembly Rooms, one of which was entitled 'The Sword of Garibaldi', with Pieroni in the chair.[148] The meetings were not well attended and there is no record of a committee being formed or subscriptions accepted.

There was great support for Garibaldi in Britain, however. After taking Sicily, in September 1860 he arrived with his troops in Naples, although he had yet to defeat the Neapolitan army on the mainland. In Britain a volunteer force was raised to go and join Garibaldi and his Redshirts. However, as the Foreign Enlistment Act made it illegal for British subjects to join the armies of foreign kings or governments, George Holyoake, who was organising the volunteers, invited them to join an excursion instead:

> A select party of English excursionists intend to visit south Italy. The excursionists will be furnished with the means of self-defence and, with a view of recognising each other, will be attired in a picturesque and uniform costume. General Garibaldi has liberally granted the excursionists a free passage to Sicily and Italy and they will be supplied with rations and clothing suitable for the climate.[149]

Pieroni's commitment to Garibaldi did not extend to him joining the excursionists; he was 41 years old by then and perhaps beyond the age of military adventure.[150] This was probably just as well, for, less than three months after they left, they were back home amid stories of disorganisation, embezzlement and a lack of military achievement.

There was, in any case, competition for military volunteers in 1860. A year earlier, the British government had created a volunteer rifle force in response to the fear, which had been growing since the Crimean War, that the country would not be well defended in the event of an invasion. The committee organising the excursionists had solicited members of the rifle volunteers to join the Italian volunteers.[151] Although Pieroni did not join the Italian volunteers he did join the English volunteers, which was taken as proof of his loyalty to Britain.

The volunteer rifle corps received much popular support, with a poem by Tennyson, 'Riflemen Form', appearing in *The Times* on 9 May. At a meeting in the Guildhall on 1 June, it was agreed to form two companies, the 1st (Bath) and the 2nd (Bathwick). By the end of June, a hundred volunteers from amongst the 'leading citizens' of Bath had joined the 1st company. Pieroni was the 132nd person to join, on 6 December 1861, when he took the following oath:

> I do sincerely promise and swear that I shall be faithful and bear true allegiance to Her Majesty Queen Victoria and that I will faithfully serve Her Majesty in Great Britain for the defence of the same against all her enemies and opposers whatsoever.[152]

He paid a one guinea enrolment fee and one guinea annual subscription, and had to provide his uniform and rifle. The rifle corps were under the control of the Lord Lieutenants of the county and each company was led by a captain. In the case of the 1st company this was Maxwell Ford.

In 1860, two 'artisan corps' were formed, the 17th (Lyncombe) and 18th (Walcot), which were made up of working-class men who could not afford to pay for their uniforms and rifles, and who were equipped from money raised by subscriptions and fundraising events. There was a strong element of class distinction in the volunteer force, as evidenced by some unpleasantness in the Lyncombe company. It was standard practice for volunteers to have some say in the choice of their officers, and the 67 men of the Lyncombe company asked for a Mr Milsom to be their lieutenant. The captain, however, refused on the grounds that he was a tradesman. Pieroni was clearly trying to establish himself above the ranks of petty tradesmen by choosing to join the 1st company.[153]

A few months after Pieroni joined, all four companies paraded so that the 2nd and 18th companies could be presented with silver bugles. The 1st company had already received a silver bugle from a Major Willocks; the bugles for the 2nd and 18th companies were bought with money raised by 'the ladies of Bath'.[154] The presentation took place in Royal Victoria Park in front of the bandstand, which was decorated with flags and a banner emblazoned with the motto 'England, Home and Beauty'. The ladies sat on the bandstand as the volunteers marched along Royal Avenue behind their fife and drum band and took up position in front of them. After a Miss Jervois had made a speech and presented the bugles, Captain Villiers of the 2nd company gave a somewhat ungracious reply complaining about the volunteers' lack of resources. His particular gripe was that the four companies were autonomous when, in his opinion, they should form a unified force. But, he admitted, it would need 600 volunteers to make this feasible and, 'though the fair women of Bath have continually proved an interest in us, the men, the idle men, have been most prominent in being backward in coming forward'. This was not, of course, true in Pieroni's case, for, despite being in his forties, he had volunteered willingly. Captain Ford of the 1st company gave a more playful speech, declaring that, 'this is the first parade of the ladies in front of the volunteers. I hope it will not be the last. Of course soldiers liked to be looked at as well as other men.' He then invited the ladies to come and watch the volunteers during their regular rifle practices, noting that modern women were taking up rifle shooting as well as the more traditional female sport of archery. The volunteers then gave three cheers for the ladies and marched to Hampton Down for manoeuvres. If Pieroni fitted the Italian stereotype, he would doubtless have appreciated the admiration of the respectable ladies of Bath.

Pieroni's membership of the volunteers did not lessen his interest in Garibaldi and the Italian question. In October 1862, he took part in a public meeting called by the mayor in support of Garibaldi. Although several well-known figures were at the meeting, others, such as Jerom Murch, the former mayor, Captain Ford of the 1st volunteer company, and William Tite were not. Nevertheless, around a thousand people attended the meeting in the Guildhall.[155] By 1862, the Kingdom of Italy had been established, although Rome was still part of the Papal States under the control of the Pope. The French had garrisoned troops in the city to prevent it being attacked by those who wanted to annexe it to the Kingdom of Italy. Garibaldi gathered a force to liberate Rome, but, in an engagement with the French, he was wounded and taken prisoner, although treated with great respect. The Bath meeting was called to show support for Garibaldi and pass a resolution urging the British government to demand that the French withdraw their forces from Rome, something the government was loath to do. The meeting also passed a resolution that the citizens of Bath, 'deeply imbued with admiration of the sublime devotion of Garibaldi to his country's cause, of the purity and simplicity of his character, most cordially sympathise with him in his recent misfortune'.

When Pieroni died in 1900, both the *Bath Chronicle* and the *Bath Journal* reported that elderly inhabitants of the city could remember when Pieroni played the part of Garibaldi in a triumphal procession 'during some festivities, and was loudly cheered'.[156] Although it has not been possible to determine when this happened, it is possible to make an educated guess. Garibaldi's celebrity in Britain continued to rise to a high pitch after 1862. After being released from prison, he returned to his home on the island of Caprera, and in 1864 paid a short visit to London. The visit generated huge enthusiasm and everyone wanted to catch a glimpse of the Italian celebrity. When he was travelling by train to Cornwall, on his way back home to Italy, his train passed through Bath. Unfortunately, most of those waiting to see him were disappointed. The day of Garibaldi's fleeting visit was also the day celebrations were being held to mark the tercentenary of Shakespeare's birth, and it is possible that, disappointed at not seeing Garibaldi, the crowd urged Pieroni to act as his stand-in during the processions planned for later in the day. Certainly there were large enthusiastic crowds around the gathering points of the Odd Fellows in the Orange Grove, the Foresters on South Parade and the Patriots in Bath Street.[157] Perhaps it was amongst the Bath Street crowd, outside his home, that Pieroni was persuaded to impersonate Garibaldi. His Italian origin, impressive build and large beard would have suited him for the role.

The extent of Pieroni's fame in mid-Victorian Bath can be gauged from a curious incident in 1860, when Elizabeth Fletcher was found guilty of 'obtaining charitable contributions under false pretences' from Fanny Mosley of Batheaston. She had knocked on Fanny's door and claimed that she was the wife of Signor Pieroni, 'who was in great distress'. She later admitted that she was the wife not of Pieroni but of one of his workmen, whom he had had to dismiss for 'intemperate habits', but still demanded money.[160]

THE TRANSIT OF GARIBALDI AND SHAKESPEARE'S TERCENTENARY
25 April 1864

Jerom Murch, the mayor of Bath, loved parades, processions and civic celebrations, a proclivity for which he was occasionally mocked.[158] For him, 25 April 1864 was a great day: in the morning Garibaldi visited Bath – albeit fleetingly – and in the afternoon the 'altar' celebrating the tercentenary of Shakespeare's birth was inaugurated in the Great Dell in Royal Victoria Park.[159]

When it became known that Garibaldi was catching a train to Fowey, where he would board the steam yacht *Ondine*, and would be passing through Bath, Murch managed to persuade the GWR to stop the train at the station for ten minutes. The plan was that Garibaldi would leave the train and go onto the footbridge which at that time linked the platform with the Royal Hotel. From there he could be seen and acclaimed by the crowds in the street below. The mayor and civic officials donned their ceremonial robes and processed from the Guildhall to the station. They were accompanied by Signor Perrugini, a singing teacher who would act as interpreter (Pieroni must have been disappointed not to have been offered the job). Large crowds had gathered at the station, all eager to see Garibaldi. Both the fashionable and the working classes were there. The numbers were swelled by the good weather and Murch's request that all the tradesmen should shut their shops and treat the day as a holiday.

The Great Western station in Bath as it looked when Garibaldi passed through

At stations all along the line crowds had gathered to see the great Italian patriot, and inevitably it was running late. Murch was notified by telegram that Garibaldi would not be able to leave the carriage when his train arrived at Bath. So, when the train arrived, Murch and his wife struggled through the crowds and managed to enter Garibaldi's compartment for a brief conversation in which he invited him to visit Bath properly and take the waters for his health. Garibaldi then opened the carriage window to wave at the crowds on the opposite platform, at which many of them swarmed onto the tracks, and he took the opportunity to shake hands with as many of the women as possible. As the train drew away from the station, the mayor had to alight quickly from the carriage, but such was the crush of people that he was lucky not to fall into the gap between the train and the platform. Crowds continued to mob the train as it made its way along the viaduct.

The day's excitement was not over, however. After lunch, the tercentenary procession began to form in various parts of the city. The highlight of the afternoon was to be the inauguration of a votive altar dedicated to Shakespeare in the Great Dell in Royal Victoria Park. The rifle volunteers, including Pieroni, assembled with their band in Queen Square. The mayoral party and the Hanoverian Band and committee gathered outside the Guildhall. Provident associations such as the Foresters, the Odd Fellows and the United Patriots, in full regalia and accompanied by brass bands, all had their allotted meeting places. The volunteers and the civic party started to process according to schedule; the plan was that they would meet up and join the provident associations in Milsom Street. The Foresters should have headed along North Parade and across North Parade Bridge before circling round via Great Pulteney Street to join the procession. However, they did not want to pay the toll to cross North Parade Bridge, so went via the Old Bridge and through Widcombe instead. This took much longer and they did not arrive in Milsom Street with the other friendly societies on time. Mr Davis, the parade organiser, wanted to wait for them, but the rifle volunteers were having no truck with a lack of military punctuality and set off marching towards Royal Victoria Park. The mayor's party also set off, but at a slower pace – even though the Hanoverian Band was playing quick marches – in the hope that the provident associations would catch them up. Eventually, they did meet up, on Royal Avenue, from where they proceeded to the Great Dell.

The Shakespeare Altar in the Great Dell, designed by CE Davis

At the dell a platform for the dignitaries had been built in front of the altar. However, no sooner had the mayor's party and the press assembled on it than it collapsed. The mayor and all fell onto their backsides but were unharmed because the platform was not that high. However, the town crier, a large, elderly man was left lying on his back shouting, 'Where is my bell? Where is my bell?', a sight which occasioned much amusement among the large crowd. Order was eventually restored, lengthy speeches were made, and in the evening there were formal dinners at which Shakespeare was quoted at length and extracts from his plays were performed.

7

THE LATTER YEARS OF PIERONI AND HIS FOUNTAIN

Pieroni's last years

Details of Pieroni's life after he gave up the licence of the Eagle Hotel are sketchy. Neither he, his home or his studio in Parsonage Lane are listed in the *Bath Post Office Directories* between 1876 and 1892. Neither does he appear in the 1881 census or burgess registers (the forerunner of electoral rolls).[161] After giving up the Eagle, he seems to have also given up modelling, allowing others to fill the gap in the market. His ex-partner and employee, William Vivian, continued working as a modeller in Chandos Buildings, and a firm of modellers called Porter & Moody operated out of 12 Parsonage Lane until 1883.

All this suggests Pieroni and his wife left Bath and returned to Italy, making only occasional return visits. Although it is not known where they stayed on these visits, one possibility is a lodging house kept by an Antonio Pieroni at 84 Avon Street. He may have been a relative, although – especially as he sometimes spelt his name Peirano – this is by no means certain.[162] He specialised in putting up Italian and other continental immigrants and it would have been an obvious place for Stefano and Rebekah to stay. In the 1881 census, among the 27 people lodging at 84 Avon Street were members of a German street brass band and some Italian musicians.[163] Avon Street had long had a reputation for gambling, prostitution and heavy drinking, although this was probably exaggerated by middle-class evangelicals who lasciviously equated poverty with vice. Although drinking, prostitution and demi-monde partying certainly went on, Avon Street was also home to many respectable working families. When Howard Goldsmid wrote a critical and salacious account of the squalor of Avon Street lodging houses in 1887, Antonio Pierano [sic] wrote an indignant letter to the *Bath Chronicle* refuting his allegations and offering to allow anyone to inspect his house from cellar to garret.[164]

There are some clues to Pieroni's whereabouts between 1876 and 1892, however. In 1880, he was in Bristol selling art objects that he had imported from Italy, so it is likely that sometime between 1876 and 1880 he had returned to Italy to buy stock. Five years later, in December 1885, he announced that he had just returned from Italy with new art works for sale, and gave his address as 12 Barton Street, Bath.[165] He made at least one more visit to Italy, and was staying in Lucca when his wife died there, aged 68, on 16 July 1888.[166] He returned to Bath after his wife's death and by 1889 had reopened his studio at 11 Parsonage Lane.[167] He may have taken it over from William Vivian, who moved to Parsonage Lane in 1888 but retired shortly afterwards.

He lived nearby at 12a Barton Street, the address he gave in 1890 when he tried to enrol on the electoral register. He seems to have changed his political allegiance, for he declared himself a Conservative, prompting the Liberals to argue that, as an alien, he was not entitled to vote. However, the revising barrister accepted Pieroni's argument that he had been naturalised 36 years previously.[168] In the 1891 census, Pieroni was recorded as occupying just two rooms at 12a Barton Street, an address he was sharing with six other people: a widow called Kezia Trebell and her son, and a house painter called Edward Lear, along with his wife and two stepsons. In 1892, he moved his workshop-cum-studio from 11 Parsonage Lane to no. 13, but continued to live at 12a Barton Street until his death. The building in Barton Street, which had been built in 1707, was demolished in the 1960s.

The building on the right, with the lamp post beside it, was 12a Barton Street, where Pieroni lived until his death in 1900. It is seen here shortly before its demolition in the 1960s.

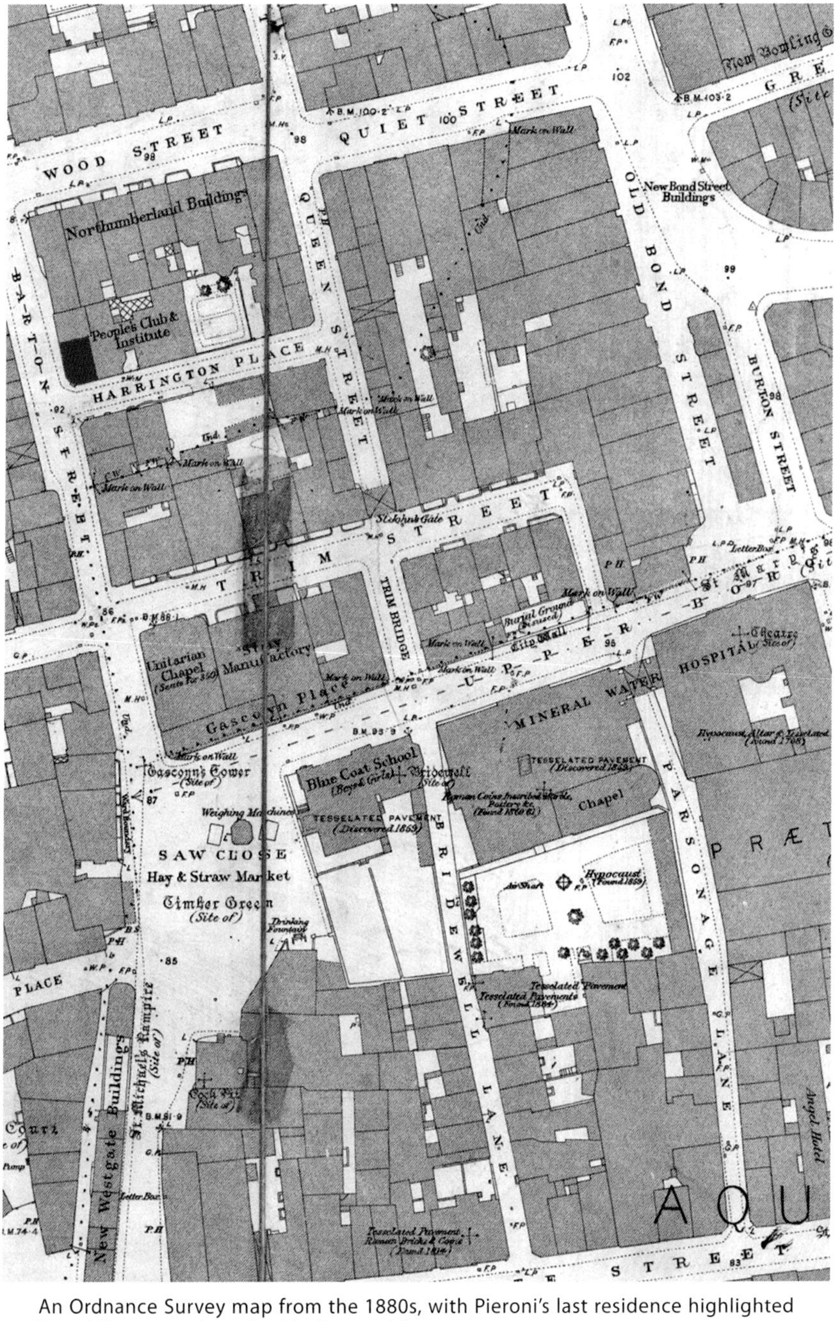

An Ordnance Survey map from the 1880s, with Pieroni's last residence highlighted in red. Parsonage Lane is at bottom right

Although, by the 1890s, Pieroni was in his seventies, he was still up for the occasional quixotic entrepreneurial venture. In 1887, Isaac Pitman, the spelling reformer and inventor of Pitman shorthand, was presented with a marble bust of himself, sculpted by Sir Thomas Brock, RA, to mark the jubilee of phonography.[169] Two years later, Pitman had a copy of the bust made in marble which he presented to the citizens of Bath. It was lodged in the Bath Royal Literary and Scientific Institute where it remains today. In 1894, when Pitman was knighted, Pieroni saw an opportunity to produce souvenirs of a local celebrity and, together with Henry Davis, he obtained the copyright of a photograph, taken by Frederick Mills, of a plaster bust of Sir Isaac.[170]

This was a typical Pieroni enterprise, involving a number of local contacts. Pieroni, Davis and Mills all had aspirations to be recognised as artists. Frederick Mills, who came from a family of market gardeners, had a photographic studio in Westgate Street and declared himself to be an artist in his publicity material.

Mills took the photograph of the plaster bust and then assigned the copyright to Pieroni and Davis. It is likely that the plaster bust, which was taken from a cast of Brock's marble bust, was made by Pieroni, even though it bore an inscription declaring it to be by Brock. A copy of the plaster bust is now in the

Thomas Brock's bust of Isaac Pitman

Details of the services offered by Frederick Mills on the back of one of his cartes de visite

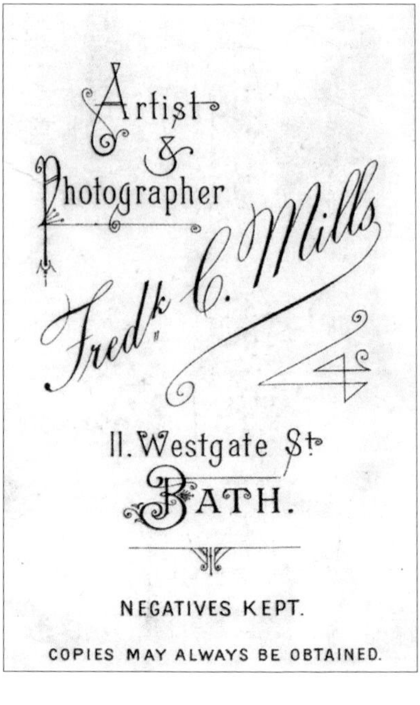

Pitman Archive at the University of Bath, along with Pitman' death mask from 1897, and these are probably the only known examples of Pieroni's modelling work to survive. Henry Davis's role in this business is unclear. He was born in Malvern in 1856 and began his working life as a house furnisher and cabinet maker. By 1886 he had married well and settled in Bath as a flower painter and 'Magnateric' cutter and engraver.[171] It is possible that his family had some connection with the Pitman family, who were well-disposed to young artists. Isaac Pitman's family came from Taunton, where Davis's mother had been in service, and this may have been the link that gave Pieroni access to Brock's bust. It is just as likely, however, that Pieroni knew Pitman from when they both worked in Parsonage Lane between 1855 and 1875. Neither Frederick Mills nor Henry Davis ultimately succeeded as artists. By 1911, Mills was a fishmonger and poultry dealer, while Davis went on to be a brewery manager and later a furniture salesman.[172]

Making a living as an artist was hard, even in a genteel place such as Bath, and it was particularly difficult for someone in his declining years like Pieroni. His last years saw a slow but inexorable descent into poverty, and he had few relations to call on. His nephew, Martin, was still in Bath, working as a 'boots' in the Weston Hotel, but his niece Maria had married Austin Bampfylde in 1871 and moved to Glamorgan.

Stefano Pieroni died on 22 February 1900, aged 83, of 'senile decay and bronchitis, at a neighbour's house, 1 Trim Street, as he was too ill to be left alone.[173] He left no will and was buried in an unmarked grave in the Catholic Cemetery at Perrymead.

The Fate of Pieroni's Fountain

The residents of Bath, then and now, have a dilemma about fountains. On the one hand they feel that as a spa city there should be magnificent and glamorous fountains; but the ones they have, or are willing to pay for, always disappoint. Bath people love writing grumbling letters to the editor of the *Bath Chronicle*. One correspondent in 2013 asked

> why there are no impressive fountains to be found in this world-renowned spa city, and how appropriate is it that one of the two or three dribblers we do have, stands over abandoned lavatories on Bog Island.[174]

Criticisms of Pieroni's fountain are nothing new, complaints having been made for almost 150 years. One of the earliest grumbles about Pieroni's fountain was voiced in a letter to the *Bath Chronicle* in 1867.[175] It was signed by 'The Inquirer', who wanted to know the answers to over twenty questions, including:

> When will the West front of the Abbey be completed? It appears to be an exceedingly tedious and difficult business?
>
> When will St Luke's church be opened?
>
> When are the new markets to be opened?
>
> When is the Banqueting Room in the Guildhall to be provided with sufficient seats? and are they to have backs?
>
> When are sufficient lamps to be erected to light the city effectively and so do away with so many 'dark corners'?
>
> When will the Police receive instructions to maintain quiet and a due regard for order in the market place on a Sunday evening?

He also wanted to know

> When is the unsightly Hot Water Fountain (!) to be removed?

Earlier the same year, at a meeting in the Guildhall, a councillor had declared the fountain to be 'a miserable thing, by which he meant that it was unsightly and was continually crumbling away'.[176] This led one wag to remark that 'the figures have got the smallpox'. He obviously did not know the legend of Bladud, who was suffering from leprosy.

Bath's ambivalent relationship with fountains can be illustrated by the history of Pieroni's fountain after its completion in 1859. In 1873, it nearly disappeared after the Surveying Committee concluded that, because of its dilapidated state and the failure to keep it supplied with mineral water, 'it had no real or ostensible purpose of either use or ornament [and] should be removed without delay'.[177] In 1859, Williams and Pieroni had only obtained an agreement to supply hot mineral water to the fountain for five years, and the supply had never been sufficient for the fountain to run continuously. Others regarded the figures of Bladud and the Four Seasons an artistic embarrassment and thought the city deserved better. The commercial classes of the lower town, who dominated the corporation, however, were never prepared to pay for better; and, as it was pointed out, they had not actually paid for the fountain which they were considering removing. The majority feeling was that the fountain should remain but that the statues should go. James Williams, who had built the fountain with Pieroni, said that, 'he would be glad, having a lingering affection for such antique relics, if the council would allow him to transport [the statues] to his residence on Entry Hill'.[178] The council agreed, and by October Bladud and the Four Seasons had been removed to their new home. A stone urn, at first loaned and then purchased, was placed on top of the fountain where Bladud had stood. The fountain enclosure was filled with potted plants that had been donated, and, rather than return them, the council decided to take on the expense of maintaining them.[179]

THE CHANGING FACE OF PIERONI'S FOUNTAIN

Pieroni's fountain stood at one of Bath's busiest junctions, and for generations of Bathonians – who could avail themselves of the mneral water that flowed freely from it – it was one of the city's most iconic landmarks. The photographs and postcards on this and the following two pages chart its fortunes – and of the city in which it stood – over a century and a half.

SILVE

Mineral Water Fountain
Bath St Bath. 1273

69 BATH. — The Mineral Water Fountain. — LL.

ARCHARD
TAILOR &
OUTFITTER &C.
FREE MINERAL WATER FOUNTAIN, BATH.

THE HOT SPRINGS FOUNTAIN, BATH.
H.880.

In 1881, the fate of the fountain came up for consideration again. This time the council decided to put a drinking fountain in front of it, to replace a public mineral-water drinking fountain that had been removed. A large slab with baroque scrolling, a basin and a tap were built in front of the fountain, and the following year iron railings were erected around the enclosure.[180] All the time, the fountain was looking more and more neglected, with so much ivy growing over it that it looked more like topiary than statuary.

Underneath the ivy, the structure of the fountain was decaying and was almost ready to come 'tumbling down', as was discovered when the ivy was removed in 1902. After the council had restored it, it was pointed out that 'the fountain ... was never the property of the Baths Committee, though they had taken compassion on it once or twice.'[181]

A year later the fountain's survival was again in question, this time because it was too close to the rails that were being laid for the new electric trams.[182] The Surveying Committee recommended its removal but some aldermen were indignant at the idea and suggested that the drinking fountain slab could just be moved instead. It was almost as through their awareness of the 'many vicissitudes' the fountain had suffered meant they did not want to interfere with it too much.[183] Indeed one councillor thought it one of the prettiest things in the city especially, as Virginia creeper was now beginning to grow up it. In the end they decided to do nothing and wait to see how things turned out when the trams started running.[184]

The fountain suffered another period of neglect after 1902, and in 1909 it was eclipsed by the installation of a new mineral water drinking fountain in the colonnade built as part of Major Davis's Empire Hotel development. Three years later, in 1912, however, the council 'took compassion on it' once again, and had it cleaned.[185]

In 1937, the fountain received a major refurbishment. The baroque drinking fountain block was replaced with an art-deco style façade with the legend 'The Hot Mineral Waters of Bath'.[188] This, it was thought, would 'bring the [fountain] into better architectural relations to the Queen's Bath and the surrounding buildings'.[189] The new fountain was set back closer to the fountain kiosk to make more space for those wanting to drink the mineral water, which was dispensed through a new stainless steel spigot. The old metal cup that had been there for many years had been replaced by two stainless steel cups on chains a few years before in 1934. The rocky outcrop on top of the fountain, on which Bladud, and later the urn, had stood, was removed, and the urn was installed on top of the kiosk. The iron railings around the fountain were also taken away so that the floral displays could be better appreciated.

A single-decker tram bound for Oldfield Park trundles past Pieroni's fountain around 1915

THE OTHER MINERAL WATER FOUNTAIN

The grand opening of the mineral water drinking fountain in the colonnade in 1909 saw a revival of the long-standing arguments over how Bath should be developed as a spa. They were the same arguments that Pieroni had come up against when building his fountain in 1859.

The purpose of the new fountain was to provide a place where mineral water could be taken in the open air, where visitors could stroll through pleasant gardens, and it was part of a drive to extend Bath's season into the spring and summer. The guest of honour at the inauguration was Sir Malcolm Morris, a noted doctor who had himself been cured of an illness by Bath's mineral water.[186] At the event, where he pressed an electric switch to start the water flowing from the new fountain, Morris was all affability and he even cracked jokes – 'Why has Bath always been considered a winter resort? Perhaps it is because we get winter days in the middle of July.' But at the luncheon at the Guildhall in front of the mayor, aldermen and town clerk he expressed some 'very candid observations':

The colonnade in the 1920s with the marble counter from which mineral water was dispensed on the left

You, the Corporation of Bath, should do your duty for the benefit of your fellow creatures, not by dawdling on year after year in your expansions, but do it, and do it quickly ... But you always think. And you talk for hours and hours upon ways and means. You spend your time considering as to whether this thing will pay or that thing will pay, and I tell you as an outside medical man you have a public duty to perform to the nation, and not to your own town only. You have no right to let millions upon millions to run to waste every summer: your duty is to use it. If the water contains some material (I know not what it is) of benefit to human beings, you have no right to let it run to waste in your river ... You have all the things to your hand here. Why on earth can't you do it, and do it properly, and at once! ... I have nothing whatever to do with Bath and its rates, or your inside petty jealousies and squabbles ... You possess – and heaven knows why you possess it, but you do possess it – the Almighty has given you a remedy for the cure of chronic diseases, and yet you don't supply a sufficient amount, and sufficient attractions for the people who should use it.

The mayor, diplomatically, hoped that the new fountain would bring to an end the long-running conflict between the corporation and the medical men. Councillor Hatt grumbled that the modern medical tourist was too keen on the 'modern requirements' available in continental spas and should be willing to accept the simple advice to bathe in Bath's mineral waters as often as they could.

The fountain was housed in an alcove in the new colonnade, with a marble counter and a marble urn from which the water was dispensed. The alcove was tiled, 'the fancy part having a green dado and a cream ground ... Light and bright tints have been chosen without being garish.'[187] The water was pumped from York Street through pipes insulated to retain its heat. One correspondent in the *Bath Chronicle* took up Morris's theme and suggested that, when the leases expired on the houses to the east of Orange Grove, they should be demolished and a grand new entrance to the Institution Gardens built. This suggestion was taken up and the result can be seen today.

The fountain seems never to have been a huge success. In 1911, it ceased to operate on Sundays because of a lack of customers. It was still in operation in 1931, although it had earlier been out of use, and stopped flowing altogether shortly after.

A sketch of the fountain by AJ Taylor, the architect who oversaw its installation

Pieroni's fountain remained in Bath Street until 1989, and was one of Bath's best-known landmarks. Edward Wells, known for his feats of long-distance walking, used it in 1888 when he undertook to walk 150 miles in three days. His route was from the fountain to the first milestone on the London road and back, which he repeated from 7am to 7 pm each day until he had achieved 50 miles.[196] In 1927, unemployed Welsh miners marching to London to protest to parliament used the fountain as a staging post. They queued up at 10am in the morning to 'partake of the waters', watched by a considerable crowd of onlookers.[197] The fountain was also a favourite pitch for local characters. In the early twentieth century, a pie man who stood there would toss coins with his customers and give them mince and meat pies for free if they won the toss, which they frequently did.[198] John Walter Carter was a shoeshine man who worked around the fountain. He was disabled and walked with a massive stick of twisted oak that made him instantly recognisable to visitors and locals.[199] The mineral waters were still popular with local people in the 1940s, and they would queue up to drink them for free at Pieroni's fountain in the belief that they was good for their rheumatism. Without the mineral water fountain they would have had to pay fourpence a glass or one shilling and sixpence a week to drink the water. When the fountain ran dry on 7 October 1946 many were alarmed, until the council admitted that no maintenance had been carried out for several years and undertook to make the repairs.[200] Suspicion that the mineral waters merely acted as a placebo, however, grew after an alleged incident at the 1924 Wembley Empire Exhibition. Bath had a pavilion at the exhibition, which included a replica of the fountain in the Pump Room, and after a woman with bad rheumatism had immersed her arm in its hot waters for a quarter of an hour, she declared her rheumatism gone. She was not to know the water was simply heated tap water and not genuine Bath spa water.[201]

The 1937 Mineral Water Drinking Fountain

The fountain was given a 'wash and brush up' in 1965 in preparation for the start of the Bath Festival, but a newspaper photograph of the spruced-up fountain shows this to have been a somewhat cursory affair, with it still looking dirty and unkempt. In 1977, the fountain was repaired by Wessex Newspapers, the owners of the *Bath Chronicle*. The following year, disaster struck when a girl died from meningitis contracted after swimming in the thermal waters, and the supply of mineral water to Pieroni's fountain was stopped.

In the 1980s, Pieroni's fountain was again threatened, but this time on aesthetic grounds. Barry Cunliffe, the archaeologist, wrote in 1986 that Bath Street was a

> brilliant piece of planning and can be enjoyed even today, even though the view from the Cross Bath is marred by the totally inappropriate Victorian fountain that stands, vulgar and askew, obscuring the view of the New Private Baths.[202]

Notice was taken, and in 1989 the fountain was dismantled, repaired, cleaned and re-erected on its present site on Bog Island between Terrace Walk and Parade Gardens. In 2009, the statue of Bladud, which had been rescued from the garden on Entry Hill and kept in storage, was erected in Parade Gardens, close to, but not in sight of its original location on top of Pieroni's fountain. This coincided with the King Bladud's Pigs project. This was a public art project in which over a hundred sculptures of pigs, individually decorated by different artists, went on display in Bath and beyond. The project provided funds for the Bath 'Two Tunnels' cycle route but also helped with the restoration of Pieroni's statue of Bladud, which now stands proudly next to a pig carved from Bath stone by Nigel Bryant.[203]

The replanting of the flower beds around Pieroni's fountain led one correspondent to the *Bath Chronicle* to propose an experiment. This grew out of the craze in the 1920s and the 1930s for radioactive radium – the most popular panacea of the time. Radium was used not only for luminescent watch and clock dials but also for decoration, toothpaste, children's atomic chemistry sets, cosmetics, and as a tonic and medicine in drinking water. Nitrogen, which had been considered the most efficacious constituent of Bath's mineral waters by the Victorians, was no longer regarded as that important. It was the radioactivity in the waters, it was claimed, that made people healthier.

The luxuriant vegetation around Pieroni's fountain – the ideal place for demonstrating the efficacy of radium, according to one correspondent in the *Bath Chronicle*

If radioactive mineral water was good for people, figured the correspondent, might it not also be good for plants. He proposed that one half of the fountain flower bed should be watered with ordinary water and the other half with mineral water, to see if 'what is good for humans might also be good for plants – and think of the splendid living advertisement.' The correspondent's pseudonym, G Randy Flora, might suggest that this was a spoof letter, but at least one reader took it seriously and replied the following week that such experiments had already been carried out.[190]

It was often claimed in the 1930s that, if people were made aware of 'the beneficial effects of regular draughts of radiumised water', they would drink more of it.[191] When the British Medical Association held its Annual Meeting in Bath in 1925 it was noted in their souvenir *Book of Bath* that the very high radium content of the natural gases had led to the development of throat and nasal sprays in which the radioactive gasses in the mineral water were atomised.[192] These sprays were administered in a special treatment room in the Queen's Baths.

In 1937 Alderman Wills, who had undertaken a fact-finding tour of British and European spas, recommended 'a great burst of enterprise of development' to revive Bath's flagging fortunes, in which the radioactivity of the city's waters would take centre stage. 'We have incomparable water with much more radioactivity in it than has been supposed,' he declared, yet 'we have never yet taken full advantage of the beneficence of nature to this city.' The main problem as he saw it, was that part of the radioactive emanations were lost between the springs and the delivery of the water to the patients. In continental spas they took, 'every possible care to prevent any escape of these emanations before they reach the patient'.[193]

An advertisement for 'Radium' Bread and a contraption for inhaling radium from 1920s guidebooks to Bath

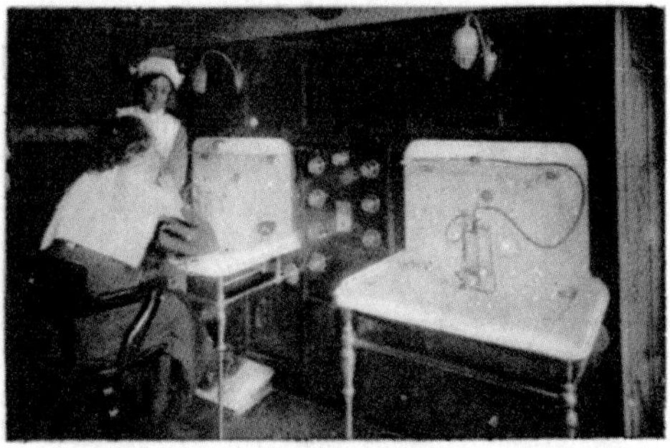

RADIUM INHALATORIUM

Yet again the paucity of fountains in the city was lamented. Wills claimed that what was needed were 'beautiful fountains such as are of great attractiveness on the continent, all illuminated at night'.[194] Pieroni's fountain was never going to meet this standard.

As early as the 1930s, however, it was known that radium could be poisonous. In 1932, the *Bath Chronicle* reported the death of a Mr Byers in America who had drunk large amounts of manufactured 'radiumised' water. The director of the Bath spa did not see this tragic occurrence as a problem, however. He pointed out that it had been caused by drinking water into which manufacturers had put too high a dose of radium, and went on to claim that 'the tragedy, sad as it is, is an unsolicited testimonial to the waters of the natural radioactive springs such as those of Bath.'[195] The radioactivity of Bath's waters was still advertised in a guidebook to the city as late as 1963, but, in the wake of the Cuban missile crisis, such references disappeared.

8

MEMORIES OF PIERONI AND HIS FOUNTAIN

Pieroni's fountain, along with other Bath fountains, symbolised a dilemma of expectations for the city. People thought, not altogether accurately, that the town's prosperity depended on attracting visitors.[204] Two main types of people were attracted to Bath. There were those who retired to Bath on a pension, often after military or colonial service, and wanted to live somewhere genteel and cheap.[205] Then there were those who visited Bath for their health or amusement, and wanted facilities and attractions similar to those in glamorous continental spas. The corporation needed to be frugal and keep down municipal and water rates to satisfy the first group, but, to encourage the second group to visit, they needed to invest ratepayers' money in developing the spa.[206] They also had to balance the competing demands of retired residents, seeking peace and quiet, and glamour-seeking visitors. In 1937, Alderman Wills argued that there was no need to invest because Bath was 'by day and night a whirlwind of gaiety' compared with continental resorts. In these, he declared, the streets were deserted by 10.30pm and most people were in bed and the lights were out. Bath did, however, lack one facility enjoyed by many continental spas – casinos. Although gambling had an impeccable eighteenth-century pedigree in Bath, Alderman Wills considered that its reintroduction would encourage 'a type of living, and a form of gaiety, which we could not, and would not desire to introduce into our city'.[207]

This tension over the role of the spa took on a political dimension because of the distribution of power in the city. The council was dominated by small businessmen from the lower town whose instincts were to keep the rates down. Plans to invest in spa projects tended to come from enthusiastic individuals, such as Pieroni, or from special interest groups such as the licensed victuallers. The lower town businessmen were familiar with managing small projects, but were averse to the risks and costs of large projects. Consequently – and in accordance with Parkinson's Law – ambitious and complex proposals, beyond their daily experience, received less attention and criticism than smaller projects such as fountains.[208] As a result, large projects such as the Pump Room Hotel of 1869, the adjacent New Royal Baths of 1867, the reconstruction of the newly discovered Roman Baths in 1897, and the Empire Hotel of 1901 – while not without

Only two other fountains grace the streets of Bath. The Rebecca Fountain in the Orange Grove (on the left) was erected in 1861 by the local temperance society on the site of a notorious inn that had recently been demolished.

The ornate fountain below was designed by Alfred Goodridge and unveiled in Laura Place in 1880. It was largely dismantled in 1949, although the basin (against which the ladder is resting) was retained, with a jet d'eau installed on top, until 1977, when it was replaced by the fountain seen inset below.

their problems and controversies – were all completed and generally admired. Smaller projects, such as fountains, on the other hand, were often mocked or abandoned and, if built, continually sniped at or neglected. Nevertheless, those who thought a spa deficient without impressive fountains continued to press for them.

The history of Bath's fountains reflects the dilemmas over what kind of city Bath wanted to be, as enthusiasm alternated with criticism. The fountain in Stall Street – both in its 1856 and 1859 incarnations – arose from initiatives by enthusiastic individuals such as Tite, Williams and Pieroni, supported by small groups of interested locals. The colonnade fountain in Institution Gardens (now renamed Parade Gardens) was the result of lobbying by the Chamber of Commerce. Municipal funds were sought to pay for both fountains but were not forthcoming and the projects had to be paid for by subscriptions or from the enthusiasts' own pockets. Other fountains, such as the Rebecca fountain – an initiative by the temperance movement – and the fountain in Laura Place, had similar origins and financing.[209] Once agreed upon, the fountains were often built cheaply and not as originally intended, as was the case with Pieroni's fountain. More ambitious projects, such as the proposed cascade of fountains from St James's Square to the obelisk in Royal Victoria Park, were never realised. Those that were built were admired by a few but were more often the butt of jokes and artistic criticism. When not the focus of scorn, Pieroni's fountain was neglected and allowed to deteriorate, losing its statues, its water supply and part of its capping, and being smothered in ivy.

Although Pieroni often referred to himself as an artist, he was not a great one. During the most active period of his career, up to the early 1870s, his attempts to gain artistic recognition in Bath were hampered by comparisons with Louis Gardie. Both were immigrants and both were in the business of modelling, figure making and art dealing . Gardie, however, had the more romantic back-story. As a young man he had volunteered for the 2nd Regiment of the Voltigeurs of Napoleon's Young imperial Guard as a sniper. He fought in the 1814 campaign and was wounded at the Battle of Laon. Later he worked as a bronze chaser – finishing cast bronze figures – for the Count D'Orsay, who, as well as being a well-known painter and sculptor, was a dandy and friend to Napoleon III. There was also a wisp of scandal about him because of his relationship with Lord Blessington, and more particularly with Blessington's wife. These relationships were given some respectability by D'Orsay's short-lived marriage to Blessington's daughter by a previous marriage. As a result, Gardie was an exotic figure in Bath, and probably better regarded as an artist. While Pieroni won a medal at the Bath Industrial Exhibition, Gardie not only won a prize at the Bristol and West of

England Exhibition but had his works displayed at the Great Exhibition in 1851 and at the Paris Exhibition of 1867. Like Pieroni, Gardie experienced periods of financial difficulty, however. He was declared bankrupt in 1856 while living in London, and, when he experienced further money problems after his retirement, his friends in Bath organised a benefit concert for him at the Assembly Rooms. The concert, which was well attended, ended with a spirited rendition of the Marseillaise.

Little of the mineral water fountain on Bog Island is Pieroni's work, as much of it belongs to the earlier fountain of 1856. The inscription that names Pieroni as its maker is faded. No busts or figures modelled by him can be identified. The busts of Captain Speke, for which he won a prize, have all disappeared. His portraits in the Victoria Art Gallery have vanished. His name on the stone tazza in Royal Victoria Park has nearly weathered away. His sole surviving work is the figure of Bladud, for which he modelled the maquette from which a monumental mason carved the statue. The statue, though, is unconvincing. The flexed right knee gives the figure an awkward stance, while the lower half of the body seems too small for the upper half. The statue's pose, which must always have been a little odd, looks even odder today because the staff Bladud is meant to be clasping is no longer there.

Stefano Pieroni died and was buried in obscurity. He and Rebekah had no children, although his nephew and niece placed an 'In memoriam' notice in the newspaper two years after his death.[210] The local newspapers reported his death and some remembered him as a colourful character. The inscription on the Bog Island fountain reads 'Stefano Vallerio Pieroni fecit'; which loosely translates as 'he made it'. He did make it, for a while, in the municipal and civic life of the city. Victorian Bath relished parades, processions, fetes, public speeches, balls and exhibitions and Pieroni found a role both as an exotic character and as a provider of the artistic accoutrements that such events required.

Pieroni's fountain also found a role in the life of the city, serving as a useful, if not greatly loved, landmark. Although neglected many times over the years and much remodelled, it still stands. I was stood by it once, photographing the inscription, when a rep from the nearby sightseeing bus stand came over and said, 'that's an interesting name. I have often wondered who he was.'

Stefano Pieroni

REFERENCES

1 C Spence, 'A Tale of Guinea Pigs', *Bath Magazine*, January 2011, p. 36.
2 SD Major, *Notabilia of Bath* (London: Hodder & Stoughton, 1871), p. 67.
3 *Bath Journal*, 10 March 1900, p. 5.
4 Pieroni's death was first reported in the *Bath Daily Chronicle and Argus*, 3 March 1900. A fuller notice was published in the *Bath Daily Chronicle and Argus*, 8 March 1900, p. 3. The same notice of Pieroni's death was included in the *Bath Weekly Chronicle*, 8 March 1900, p. 5.
5 *Bath Weekly Chronicle*, 13 April 1893, p. 6.
6 *Bath Weekly Chronicle and Herald*, 17 September 1949, p. 16.
7 Ibid.
8 *Bath Weekly Chronicle*, 8 March 1900, p. 5.
9 *Bath Weekly Chronicle*, 4 May 1899 & 31 May 1900; A Graves A, *The Royal Academy of Arts: A Complete Dictionary of Contributors and their work from its Foundation in 1769 to 1904*, vol. III (London: Henry Graves & Co and George Bell & Sons, 1905), p. 30.
10 Email to the author from Victoria Art Gallery.
11 *Bath Weekly Chronicle*, 14 December 1899; *Bristol Mercury & Daily Post*, 2 June 1900.
12 *Bath Weekly Chronicle*, 22 November 1866, p. 7.
13 Census 1871, piece 2480, folio 36, p. 25; P Malone, 'An Italian Legacy', *Bath Magazine*, January 2013, p. 30.
14 1881 census, piece 2474, folio 74, p. 6; *Kellys Directory of Somerset with the City of Bristol*, 1889, p. 245; J Wright & Co, *Directory of Bristol* 1901.
15 Marriage certificates of Stefano Pieroni and Pietro Pieroni.
16 *Penny Magazine*, 2 February 1833, no. 54, pp 42-43.
17 *Penny Magazine*, p. 42.
18 Paola A Sensi-Isolani, *Italian Image makers in France, England and the United States* (1990) <http://www.fazzi.nl/figurusti-di-gesso/fazzi/italian_image_makers.htm.
19 *Penny Magazine*, pp. 42-43
20 Records of alien arrivals & certificates of arrival; available on Ancestry.co.uk.
21 Ibid.
22 AR Flaten, *Medals and Plaquettes in the Ulrich Middledorf Collection at the Indiana University Art Museum* (Bloomington: University of Indiana Press, 2012).
23 *Morning Chronicle*, 28 July 1855, p. 3.
24 L Sponza, *Italian Immigrants in Nineteenth-century Britain: Realities and Images* (Leicester: Leicester University Press, 1988).
25 1841 census. The search for Pieroni in the census was done using the digital databases available on both ancestry.co.uk and Findmypast.co.uk.
26 National Portrait Gallery, *British Bronze Sculpture Founders and Plaster-figure Makers, 1800-1980* <http://www.npg.org.uk/research/programmes/plaster-figure-makers-history.php.
27 *Birmingham Daily Post*, 5 May 1859.
28 *Belfast News Letter*, 25 May 1876.
29 <http://www.heritagecity.org/research-centre/whos-who/giovanni-bianchi.htm. Site accessed 12 June 2011.
30 Sponza, op. cit.
31 Although her name was spelt Rebekah on the marriage certificate, in census returns for 1861 and 1871, when she was living in Bath, she appears as Rebecca. It is unclear, however, whether she decided to change the spelling of her name or whether the census enumerators used the English spelling by default.
32 *Bath Post Office Directories* for 1849, 1850 & 1852.
33 Malone, op. cit.
34 National Portrait Gallery, op. cit.
35 Stefano Pieroni, naturalisation papers; National Archives, HO1/ 84/2649/ C428067.
36 1851 census, HO 107, piece 1941, folio 240, 69.

37 A Swift and K Elliott, *Literary Walks in Bath: Eleven Excursions in the Company of Eminent Authors* (Bath: Akeman Press, 2012), pp. 186-187.

38 *Bath Post Office Directory* 1854, p. 493.

39 *Bath Weekly Chronicle*, 13 April 1893, p. 6. The official name of the rooms was the Commercial & Literary Institution. It was founded in 1847 and provided rooms for chess, reading and classes. After it moved from Upper Borough Walls it was based in Post Office Chambers, York Buildings; Major, op.cit., p. 20.

40 The *Bath Directories* from 1854 to 1876 locate the workshop within Parsonage Lane without giving a street number.

41 *Kelly's Directory of Somerset & Bristol*, 1889, pp. 592, 69.

42 Cotterell's map shows the numbering sequence of Parsonage Lane to begin at the southern end on the eastern side and not on the western side as it does now. Unfortunately the map does not show the sequence for the western side of the lane. However it does show the numbers for the adjacent Bridewell Lane which go from 1-11 running north and then 15-22 running south down the western side. If this same system was used for Parsonage Lane then it is quite possible that the current No 1 was No 13 in Victorian times. Pieroni must have moved into No 13 sometime after 1870 because, before that date, it was a warehouse occupied by Charles Shepherd (1850-1862) and then by Isaac White (1864-1870): Parish Rate Books.

43 Meg Hamilton, *Bath Before Beau Nash* (Bath: Kingsmead Press), 1978, p 54.

44 B Pitman, *Isaac Pitman: His Life and Labours Told and Illustrated by Benn Pitman* (Cincinnati: CJ Krehbial & Co, 1902), pp. 124-125.

45 TA Reed, *Biography of Isaac Pitman, Inventor of Phonography* (London: Griffith, Farran, Okeden & Welsh, 1887), p. 114.

46 *Bristol Mercury*, 22 March 1862.

47 *Bath Weekly Chronicle*, 25 August 1859.

48 *Bristol Mercury*, 8 April 1865.

49 Email from Peter Malone. The casts are now stored in the chapel of the Abbey Cemetery.

50 Vivian's name had been anglicised from the Italian Viviani, but he had been born in Haverfordwest, hence the Welsh element in his name.

51 *Wells Journal*, 11 September 1858, p. 8.

52 *Wells Journal*, 26 September 1858.

53 *Bristol Mercury and Daily Post*, 17 September 1888.

54 *The Times*, 17 September 1864, p. 12.

55 T Jeal, *Explorers of the Nile: The Triumph and Tragedy of a Great Victorian Adventure* (London: Faber & Faber, 2011).

56 *Bath Weekly Chronicle*, 17 October 1867, p. 7.

57 *Bath Weekly Chronicle*, 22 September 1854.

58 University of Glasgow, 'Louis Gardie: Mapping the Practice and Profession of Sculpture in Britain and Ireland 1851-1951', *History of Art and HATII* <http://sculpture.gla.ac.uk/view/person.php?id=msib7_1206620114, accessed 14 Jan 2013. Census 1861, RG 09, piece 1686, folio 41, p. 29. Gardie was still living in Westgate Buildings in 1871: Census piece 2480, folio 39, page 32.

59 *Bristol Mercury*, 12 November 1864.

60 *Bath Weekly Chronicle*, 13 October 1864, p. 8; 20 October 1864, p. 8; 3 November 1864, p. 8; 10 November 1864, p. 8.

61 *Bath Weekly Chronicle*, 18 May 1865; 8 June 1865, p. 5.

62 *Bath Weekly Chronicle*, 29 December 1864, p. 3; 12 January 1865.

63 <http://www.bonhams.com/auctions/17860/lot/243/; National Portrait Gallery Collections, *Bust of John Hanning Speke* <http://www.npg.org.uk/collections/search/portrait/mw05940/John-Hanning-Speke.

64 R Bridges, 'John Hanning Speke (1827–1864)', *Oxford Dictionary of National Biography*, Oxford University Press, 2004 <http://www.oxforddnb.com/view/article/26101, accessed 14 Jan 2013.

65 Email to the author from the Royal Albert Memorial Museum, 14 January 2013.

66 W Carr, 'John Hanning Speke', *Dictionary of National Biography 1885-1900*, vol. 53; email to the author from Jan Turner of the Royal Geographical Society,17 January 2013.

67 Email to the author from the Rev Geoff Wade, Vicar of St Andrews Church. He says that a NADFAS survey of the church, dated 1991, records the bust as of marble.

68 I Burton, 'Who Lasts Wins', *Frazer's Magazine,* 1869.

69 *London Gazette*, 5 May 1863, p. 2436; the name Line is mistranscribed as Liou.

70 Sponza, op. cit., p. 77.

71 M Chapman, 'Bath and the Ornamental Fountain', *The Survey of Bath and District*, 22 (October, 2007), pp. 45-53.

72 Op. cit p. 47.

73 Op. cit. & J Lees-Milne & D Ford, *Images of Bath* (Richmond: St Helena Press, 1982); the reference is to the carvings on the abbey's west front known as Bishop Oliver's Dream which show angels ascending a ladder.

74 *Bath Weekly Chronicle*, 17 January 1856.

75 *Bath Weekly Chronicle*, 8 May 1856.

76 *Bath Weekly Chronicle*, 5 June 1856.

77 *Bath Weekly Chronicle*, 3 July 1856.

78 William Parker, *New Physiological Views with an Appendix on the Bath Thermal Waters, with a Frontispiece of the Bath Mineral Water Fountain* (Bath, Peach, 1856).

79 *Bath Weekly Chronicle*, 12 August 1856.

80 *Bath Weekly Chronicle*, 5 November 1857, p. 6: 26 November 1857.

81 *Bath Weekly Chronicle*, 29 October 1857, p. 3.

82 Parker op. cit. pp. 21-23.

83 *Bath Weekly Chronicle*, 13 September 1855, p. 3.

84 RW Falconer, *The Baths and the Mineral Waters of Bath*, 6th ed. (Bath: Peach, 1880), pp. 34-37.

85 *Bath Weekly Chronicle*, 18 November 1858, p. 2.

86 *Bath Weekly Chronicle*, 11 November 1858, p. 3.

87 *Bath Weekly Chronicle*, 2 December 1858, p. 3.

88 G Davis, (2009) *Bath as Spa and Bath as Slum* (Lampeter: Edwin Mellen Press, 2009), p. 12.

89 *Bath Weekly Chronicle*, 11 April 1859.

90 *Bath Weekly Chronicle*, 28 April 1859.

91 *Bath Weekly Chronicle*, 28 April 1859.

92 *Bath Journal*, 16 April 1859.

93 *Bath Weekly Chronicle* 28 April 1859, p. 5.

94 Anstey was the author of *The New Bath Guide*, published in 1766, a verse satire of Georgian Bath that remained popular, and continued to be published, well into Victorian times. A modern edition, with an introduction by Gavin Turner was published by Broadcast Books, Bristol in 1994. He also composed a satirical poem called *The Election Ball*, which was not particularly political in its satire.

95 RE Peach, *The Bath Poll Book 1859* (Bath: Peach, 1859).

96 *Bath Weekly Chronicle*, 26 May 1859; Minutes of the Hot Water Fountain Committee, 16 May 1859; Minutes of the Bath Act Committee, 23 May 1859; Minutes of the Baths and Pump Room Committee, 26 May 1859, Bath Record Office.

97 P Borsay, *The Image of Georgian Bath 1700-2000* (Oxford: Oxford University Press, 2008), p. 67; J Earle, *A Guide to the Knowledge of Bath, Ancient and Modern*, (London, 1864) (quoted in Borsay).

98 B Cunliffe, *The City of Bath* (Gloucester: Alan Sutton, 1986), p. 160.

99 Minutes of the Pump Room and Baths Committee, 17 November 1859, Bath Record Office. The hole in the ceiling of the vault under Stall Street through which the fountain was fed with mineral water can still be seen.

100 *Bath and Cheltenham Gazette*, 23 November 1859; clipping in the *Hunt Collection*, vol. 1, p. 261, Bath Central Library.

101 Newspaper cutting, 7 December 1859 in the *Hunt Collection*, vol. 1, p. 261, Bath Central Library.

102 *Bath Weekly Chronicle*, 22 December 1859.

103 *Bath Journal*, 10 December 1859, p. 4.

104 *Bath Weekly Chronicle*, 15 December 1859.

105 *An Appeal to the Nobility, Gentry and Citizens of Bath on Behalf of the Builders of the New Hot-Water Fountain in Bath Street with a List of Subscribers, etc* (Bath: J Francis, Kingsmead St, 1860). bound with *Falconers's Tracts,* Local History Section, Bath Central Library.

106 Minutes of the Baths and Pump Room Committee Meeting, 1 July 1860, Bath Record Office.

107 *Bath Weekly Chronicle*, 14 August 1873, p. 3.
108 *Bath Chronicle*, 8 December 1859, p. 5.
109 Census 1861, RG09, piece 1686, folio 31, p. 9.
110 *Bath Weekly Chronicle*, 22 August 1867, p. 8.
111 *Bath Weekly Chronicle*, 8 February, 1866.
112 *Bath Weekly Chronicle*, 5 September 1867, p. 8.
113 *Bath Weekly Chronicle*, 17 October 1867.
114 *Bath Weekly Chronicle*, 27 August 1868.
115 See 'Notes by the Way' in the *Bath Weekly Chronicle and Herald*, 17 September 1949, 16.
116 Census 1871, RG10, piece 2480, folio 25, p. 4.
117 *Bath Weekly Chronicle*, 27 November 1873.
118 *Bristol Mercury*, 22 October 1870.
119 *Western Daily Press*, 23 July 1875, p. 4.
120 *Western* Daily Press, 11 October 1875, p. 3. See also Bristol's Lost Pubs <www. bristolslost pubs.eu.page215.html; Census 1881 RG11, piece 2436, folio 34, p. 25.
121 *Exeter Flying Post*, 28 October 1858; *Western Times*, 28 November 1858, p. 1.
122 *Bristol Mercury*, 22 January 1859.
123 *Worcestershire Chronicle*, 13 July 1859, p. 3.
124 *Bath Weekly Chronicle*, 22 May 1862.
125 *Bath Weekly Chronicle*, 2 June 1864. p. 4; 27 April 1865, p. 4.
126 *Bristol Mercury*, 31 August 1880, p. 1.
127 *Bath Weekly Chronicle*, 24 December 1885; 31 December 1885; 7 January 1886.
128 *Bath Weekly Chronicle*, 19 July 1860, p. 5; the story of the Victoria Park statuary is also told in Chapman, op.cit.
129 *Bath Weekly Chronicle*, 2 May 1861; Chapman op. cit.
130 *Bath Weekly Chronicle*, 11 July 1861, p. 8.
131 *Bath Weekly Chronicle*, 8 June 1854, p. 2.
132 *Bath Weekly Chronicle*, 22 December 1861.
133 *Western Daily Press*, 4 April 1872, p. 3.
134 B Snaddon, *The Last Promenade: Sydney Gardens Bath*, (Bath, Millstream Books, 2000), p. 43.
135 *Bath Weekly Chronicle*, 20 May 1858.
136 *Bath Weekly Chronicle*, 20 May 1858.
137 *Bristol Mercury*, 8 September 1860.
138 *Bath Weekly Chronicle*, 6 September, 1860, p. 5.
139 *Bath Weekly Chronicle*, 15 September 1860, p. 5.
140 *Bristol Mercury*, 8 April 1865.
141 *Bath Weekly Chronicle*, 19 May 1864, p. 7.
142 *Bath Weekly Chronicle*, 22 November 1866, p. 7.
143 *Bath Weekly Chronicle*, 15 August 1867, p. 3; 17 October 1867, p. 7.
144 *Taunton Courier and Western Advertiser*, 16 August 1865, pp. 6-7; *Bristol Mercury*, 12 August 1865.
145 *Bath Weekly Chronicle*, 17 September 1949, p. 16.
146 *Bath Weekly Chronicle* 27 February 1868, p. 4; 20 February 1868, p. 4.
147 Anon, *Memorie Dei Toscana alla Guerra del 1848* (Firenze: Firenze Tipografia Nazionale Italiano, 1952), p. 39.
148 *Bath Weekly Chronicle*, 21 July 1860, p. 3.
149 W Cope Devereux, *Fair Italy, the Riviera and Monte Carlo* (London: Kegan, Paul & Trench, 1884), appendix 1.
150 Email from Emma Cresswell, Raphael Samuel Project Archivist, The Bishopgate Institute. The Institute has a card index of the members of the excursionists, and Pieroni is not in it. The Institute holds the Holyoake Papers that refer to the excursionists.
151 MC Finn, *After Chartism: Class and nation in English Radical Politics, 1848-1874* (Cambridge: Cambridge University Press, 1993), pp. 207-208, fn. 56.
152 Roll of the 1st Bath Company of the Somersetshire Volunteer Rifles, Somerset Record Office, DD/SL1 3/2/20.
153 WG Fisher, *A History of the Somerset Yeomanry, Voluntary and Territorial Forces* (Taunton: Phoenix Press, 1924).
154 *Bath Weekly Chronicle*, 26 September, 1861, p. 3; *Bath Weekly Chronicle*, 24 April 1862, p. 3; *Somerset and Wiltshire Journal*, 26 April 1862, p. 4.
155 *Bath Weekly Chronicle*, 16 October 1862, p. 3; *Somerset & Wilts Journal*, 25 October 1862, p. 4.
156 *Bath Chronicle*, 8 March 1900, p. 5; *Bath Journal*, 10 March 1900, p. 5.
157 *Bath and Cheltenham Gazette*, 27 April 1864, p. 4.
158 *Bath Weekly Chronicle*, 29 October 1868: letter from 'Vespertilio' in response to a

torchlight parade with Chinese lanterns organised by Murch to welcome the two Liberal candidates in the General Election to Bath (see *Bath Weekly Chronicle*, 22 October 1868).

159 *Bath Journal*, 30 April 1864, pp. 6-8; *Bath Weekly Chronicle*, 28 April, 1864.

160 *Bath Weekly Chronicle*, 20 September 1860, p. 3.

161 *Registers of Bath Electors*, Bath Record Office.

162 For example Antonio appears as living at 84 Avon Street in both the 1880 and the 1885 *Bath Burgess Rolls*; but in 1880 he is recorded as Peirano and in 1885 as Pierano. On his 1858 marriage certificate he is Periano but his will is recorded in the *National Probate Calendar* under the name Pieroni, even though he left the lodging house to his wife Sarah Peirano.

163 Census 1881, RG 11/2441, pp. 33-34.

164 Davis op. cit. pp. 259-260.

165 *Bath Weekly Chronicle*, 24 December 1885, p. 4; 31 December 1885, p. 4; 7 January 1886, p. 8.

166 *Bath Weekly Chronicle*, 26 July 1888, p. 5.

167 *Kelly's Directory of Somerset and Bristol*, 1889, pp. 69, 592. Available at Ancestrry.co.uk.

168 *Bath Weekly Chronicle*, 11 September 1890, p. 3.

169 Reed, op. cit.

170 National Archives, Copyright registration. Records of the Copyright Office, Stationers' Company, COPY 1/417/504.

171 Census 1891, RG12, piece 1931, folio 98, p. 8. Electro-magnetic engraving was a process by which a facsimile engraved plate could be made from a drawing by using a form of pentigraph in conjunction with a non-conducting ink on an electrically conducting surface. Electro-magnets would cause the engraving tool to scribe as the ink on the original activated the magnets. See 'Hansen's electro-magnetic engraving machine', *Philosophical Magazine,*Series, 4, vol. 7, issue 48 (1854), pp. 527-528.

172 Census 1901 RG13, piece 2781, folio 143, p. Census 1911.

173 Death certificate for SV Pieroni.

174 *Bath Chronicle*, 28 February 2013, p. 45.

175 *Bath Weekly Chronicle*, 21 November 1867.

176 *Bath Weekly Chronicle*, 9 May 1867, p. 8.

177 Minutes of a Special Meeting of the Spa Committee, 24 April 1873, p. 313, Bath Record Office.

178 Chapman, op. cit., p. 51; *Bath Weekly Chronicle,* 15 May 1873, p. 3.

179 *Bath Weekly Chronicle,* 16 October 1873, p. 3.

180 *Bath Weekly Chronicle*, 18 August 1881, pp. 7; 5 January 1882, p. 7.

181 Meeting of the Pleasure Grounds Committee, *Bath Weekly Chronicle,* 10 April 1902, p. 2.

182 *Bath Weekly Chronicle*, 24 September 1903, p. 2.

183 *Bath Weekly Chronicle*, 24 September 1903, p. 5.

184 *Bath Weekly Chronicle*, 19 November 1903, p. 2.

185 *Bath Chronicle and Weekly Gazette*, 6 July 1912, p. 7.

186 Anon, *Bath: Opening of the Mineral Water Fountain and Colonnade in the Institution Gardens, by Sir Malcolm Morris, KCVO, FRCS*, (Bath, 1909), Bath Central Library.

187 *Bath Chronicle and Weekly Gazette*, 10 June 1909. p. 6.

188 This is still preserved in the stone store of the Roman Baths Museum. *Bath Weekly Chronicle & Herald*, 4 August 1934, p. 21; 12 June 1937, p. 7; 24 July 1937, p. 12.

189 Report of the Spa Committee, Jan-March 1937; City of Bath Council and Committee Minutes 1937, p. 414, Bath Record Office.

190 *Bath Weekly Chronicle and Herald*, 24 July 1937.

191 *Bath Weekly Chronicle and Herald,* 27 May 1933, p. 7.

192 *The Book of Bath, written for the 93rd Annual Meeting of the British Medical Association held in Bath in July 1925* (Bath: 1925), p. 119.

193 A report by AW Wills on his Visit to Continental Spas, Minutes of the Spa Committee, 19 October 1937, p. 896, Bath Record Office.

194 *Bath Weekly Chronicle & Herald*, 23 October 1937, p. 4.

195 *Bath Weekly Chronicle & Herald*, 9 April 1932, p. 11.

196 *Bristol Mercury & Daily Post*, 6 November 1888.
197 *Bath Weekly Chronicle & Herald*, 12 November 1927, p. 25.
198 *Bath Weekly Chronicle & Herald*, 28 July 1934, p. 21.
199 *Bath Weekly Chronicle & Herald*, 27 January 1945, p. 1.
200 *Bath Weekly Chronicle & Herald*, 12 October 1946, p. 2.
201 *Bath Weekly Chronicle & Herald*, 12 September 1925, p. 8.
202 B Cunliffe, op.cit.
203 *King Bladud's Pigs in Bath* <http://www.kingbladudspigs.org/index.html; <http://news.bbc.co.uk/local/bristol/hi/people_and_places/history/newsid_8325000/8325946.stm.
204 Davis, op. cit.
205 Davis, op. cit. pp. 29-31.
206 Davis, op.cit. pp. 31-32.
207 A Report by AW Wills on his Visit to Continental Spas, Minutes of the Spa Committee 19 October 1937, p. 896, Bath Record Office.
208 C Northcote Parkinson, *Parkinson's Law, or The Pursuit of Progress* (London: John Murray, 1958); the negative attitude to small-scale projects may explain why Mr Lansdown, the Southgate Street jeweller, refused to pay his share of the costs of the Tite fountain.
209 Chapman, op. cit. pp. 52-53.
210 *Bath Weekly Chronicle*, 7 February 1902.

PICTURE CREDITS

Bath Record Office, 14, 39 (bottom), 59, 69; Bridgeman Art Library, 7, 50; Christopher Wheeler 34, 56 and cover; National Portarit Gallery, 19; Bath in time/Bath Reference Library 23, 25, 31, 45 (top), 70.

Other illustrations are from the collection of Colin Fisher or the Akeman Press Archive.

ACKNOWLEDGEMENTS

Stefano Pieroni left behind him no archives and no correspondence. Until recently this would have made researching his life impossible, because the only references to him were scattered and uncatalogued throughout many public records and newspaper archives. The task has become possible because the internet and the digitisation of archives has made searching for metaphorical needles in archival haystacks possible. The main online resources used were:

The British Newspaper Archive: brightsolid/ British Library
Bathintime.co.uk
Access 2 Archives
The Public Record Office online catalogue
Ancestry.co.uk
Findmypast.co.uk
The London Gazette Online

When I started this project I made the mistake of thinking that, because the subject was obscure, I would be alone in researching it. This was a naïve assumption, as the history of Bath has been hugely studied. Mike Chapman had done much work on the fountains of Bath and Peter Malone has done much work on Italian plaster-figure makers, including Pieroni. I hope I have managed to add a little to the work they have already done.

Real, rather than virtual, archival resources are still important, and thanks are due to the helpful people at the Local Studies Collection at Bath Central Library, Bath Record Office and Somerset Record Office.

Thanks also to Andrew Swift for his editorial and design work and especially for sourcing some fascinating illustrations.

INDEX